PROPERTY VALUATION
AND ACCOUNTS

PROPERTY VALUATION
AND
ACCOUNTS

C A WESTWICK
B.Sc. (ECON), F.C.A.
*(Research Fellow, London School of Economics,
Former Technical Director,
The Institute of Chartered Accountants in England and Wales)*

The Institute of Chartered Accountants
in England and Wales
Chartered Accountants' Hall, Moorgate Place
London EC2P 2BJ
1980

© 1980 C. A. Westwick, Richard Ellis, Dearden Farrow
ISBN 0 85291 254 4

Other Publications by C. A. Westwick:

A study of profitability in the hosiery and knitwear industry,
National Economic Development Office, 1971.
Accuracy of profit forecasts in bid situations,
Institute of Chartered Accountants in England and Wales, 1972.
Investment appraisal for the clothing industry, HMSO, 1973.
Accounting for inflation: A working guide to the accounting procedures,
Institute of Chartered Accountants in England and Wales, 1973.
How to use management ratios, Gower Press, 1973.
Investment Appraisal and Inflation, Research Committee Occasional Paper No. 7.
Institute of Chartered Accountants in England and Wales, 1976 (with P. S. D. Shohet).

This book is based on research sponsored by
Richard Ellis, Chartered Surveyors, and
Dearden Farrow, Chartered Accountants

This book is composed in Baskerville 11pt on 12 with 9pt on 10; printed and bound by Heffers Printers Ltd., Cambridge

Contents

Abbreviations

A.S.C.	Accounting Standards Committee
C.A.	Companies Act
C.C.A.	Current Cost Accounting
C.G.T.	Capital Gains Tax
C.S.O.	Central Statistical Office
D.L.T.	Development Land Tax
D.R.C.	Depreciated Replacement Cost
E.D.	Exposure Draft
G.R.C.	Gross Replacement Cost
O.M.V.	Open Market Value
R.I.C.S.	Royal Institution of Chartered Surveyors
S.S.A.P.	Statement of Standard Accounting Practice

ix

Introduction

Objectives of book

The objectives of this book are to explore the problems associated with incorporating a valuation of its property in the annual report of a manufacturing or trading company. Property companies are specifically excluded. This book is addressed to businessmen, accountants, auditors, valuers, and all those who make use of published accounts. Its aim is to increase the understanding of members of each of these groups of the needs and problems of the members of the other groups, with a view to contributing to the process of improving the value of published accounts to their users.

Acknowledgements

This book is largely based on material prepared for, and the discussion which took place at, a joint seminar attended by senior members of the staffs of Richard Ellis, Chartered Surveyors, and Dearden Farrow, Chartered Accountants, which I chaired in March 1979. Those attending are listed in Appendix 7. I should like to congratulate these two firms for their initiative in proposing the seminar and to thank all who took part for their useful contributions.

I should especially like to thank Tim Roberton of Richard Ellis and Jo Holden of Dearden Farrow for their invaluable comments on earlier drafts. As well as generously financing the research and writing of this book, Richard Ellis and Dearden Farrow gave me unfettered access to their records (subject of course to client confidentiality). These contributions have helped immensely to give this book the practical flavour which we hope it has, and to make it of practical value to users, producers and auditors of accounts, and to valuers.

I am grateful to Professor Harold Edey and to John Rule for helpful comments on the draft.

I should also like to thank Mrs Lise-Lotte Neale of Dearden Farrow for her painstaking work on analysing published accounts, and Mrs Barbara Piper of Richard Ellis for typing so patiently the various drafts of this book.

I am grateful to the following for permission to reproduce the material indicated:

The Institute of Chartered Accountants in England and Wales: Extracts from the *Survey of Published Accounts 1978,* extracts from *The Private Shareholder and the Corporate Report* by T. A. Lee and D. P. Tweedie, *Valuations of Company Property Assets and their Disclosure in Directors' Reports or Accounts of Companies* — Statement S20 from the Institute's Members' Handbook, *Disclosure of Accounting Policies* (Statement of Standard Accounting Practice No. 2) and *Accounting for Depreciation* (Statement of Standard Accounting Practice No. 12).

Allen and Unwin:
Extracts from *The Economics of Real Property* by R. Turvey.

The Royal Institution of Chartered Surveyors:
Valuation of Company Property Assets, Guidance Note No. A2, and *Guidance Notes on the Valuation of Plant and Machinery,* Guidance Note No. F2.

The Council of the Stock Exchange:
Chapter 6 of the 'Yellow Book'.

C. A. WESTWICK

London
March 1980

I

The use of valuations

1 Situations in which a valuation may be used or required

There are many situations in which a valuation of a company's property may be used or required. Table 1 shows the principal situations but in this book we shall be primarily concentrating on (a) Annual accounts, and to a lesser extent on (b) to (f), and only in passing to (g) to (k).

Table 1

Situations in which a capital valuation may be used and/or required.

a. Annual Accounts.
   i. Companies Act 1967.
   ii. Current Cost Accounts (SSAP16).
b. Company borrowing (e.g. debenture).
c. Valuation of a non-listed company for share transfer purposes.
d. Takeover bids.
e. Flotation.
f. Capital reorganisation.
g. Insurance.
h. Liquidations, bankruptcy, receiverships.
i. Taxation.
   i. Development Land Tax.
   ii. Capital Gains Tax.
   iii. Capital Transfer Tax.
   iv. Stamp Duty.
j. Compulsory acquisition.
k. Special cases (e.g. Insurance Companies and Property Investment Companies).

Nevertheless Table 1 is a useful reminder of the many situations in which businessmen, accountants, auditors and valuers will be involved together with the valuation of a company's property, and when it will be important that each should have an understanding of the others' needs, the extent of their abilities, any limitations of their techniques and of the special meaning which they are giving to words.

2 Who are the users of published accounts?

It will be useful throughout the discussion in this book to remind ourselves who are the customers for our product — who are the users of published accounts — because it is their needs for information which we are trying to satisfy. The Corporate Report published as a discussion document by the Accounting Standards Committee gives the following list of users of published accounts:

(a) *The equity investor group* including existing and potential shareholders and holders of convertible securities, options or warrants.

(b) *The loan creditor group* including existing and potential holders of debentures and loan stock, and providers of short term secured and unsecured loans and finance.

(c) *The employee group* including existing, potential and past employees.

(d) *The analyst-adviser group* including financial analysts and journalists, economists, statisticians, researchers, trade unions, stockbrokers and other providers of advisory services such as credit rating agencies.

(e) *The business contact group* including customers, trade creditors and suppliers and in a different sense competitors, business rivals, and those interested in mergers, amalgamations and takeovers.

(f) *The government* including tax authorities, departments and agencies concerned with the supervision of commerce and industry, and local authorities.

(g) *The public* including taxpayers, ratepayers, consumers, and other community and special interest groups such as political parties, consumer and environmental protection societies and regional pressure groups.

Of all these users we shall be most concerned with the equity investor, the loan creditor, the analyst-adviser, the business contact and the employee groups.

3   **What do the users of published accounts want from a property valuation?**

The equity investor and long-term lender
The equity investor and the long term lender to the company will want to see how, and how well, the directors have used their money. The company's balance sheet will show how the money has been used because, at the date on which it is drawn up, it sets out from where the company has obtained finance (the equity shareholders in the shape of subscribed capital and retained profits, the government in the shape of deferred tax and grants, the debenture holder, the company's bank, and its trade creditors) and in what that finance has been invested (land, buildings, plant, machinery, vehicles, stock, debtors, and cash).

The original, historical cost of the property will adequately answer the question 'How has the money been used', but with inflation and changes in property values, the property's historical cost will, after a few years, fail to answer the question 'How well has the property been used'. To answer that question an up-to-date value is needed in order to show to what extent the property has kept its original value or has risen in value faster or slower than general inflation.

Such changes in value would, for a non-property company, be regarded as windfall gains or losses and only in exceptional circumstances would they lead to management or shareholder action. But a more frequent and usual reason for a user of accounts wanting to know what is the up-to-date value of a company's property is in order to calculate the company's return on capital in order to assess how well the business is being run. Return on capital is of course not the only way of measuring a company's efficiency but it is the method which is most dependent on property valuations.

Return on capital
At first sight it might appear to be unreasonable to calculate a return on capital ratio based on current values when the capital which was originally invested is the historical cost of the asset concerned. But there are two reasons why current values are needed. Firstly as a result of inflation, the £ today in which profit is measured is of a very different value to the £ in which the property's original cost was measured, and to divide these two kinds of pounds has been described as like dividing coconuts by peanuts and calling the answer nuts.

The second reason is that if a company cannot earn an adequate

5

return on the current value of its property, then it may be better for the shareholders to realise the capital appreciation on the property by selling it and for the company to move to a cheaper location, subject of course to the magnitude of any disruption costs associated with such a move. The benefit of a wise purchase of property some years ago may be recouped by remaining in it, but sometimes it will only be realised by selling up and moving on. If the property is sold then the company may be liable to corporation tax on the 'capital gain' — the difference between the original cost, (or the value at 6th April, 1965 if owned then), and the sales proceeds. This tax may be deferred by roll-over relief. The amount of the exposure to deferred tax for revaluations and roll-over should be shown in the notes to the accounts (SSAP 15 paras 19 and 33).

Although various return on capital ratios are frequently used to assess the efficiency of a company's management, it must be acknowledged that these ratios have limitations in addition to the frequent lack of up-to-date valuations of property and other fixed assets. For example:

(1) Profit figures may not be comparable between companies despite the work of the Accounting Standards Committee, as a result of differences in the treatment of overseas operations, research and development, pension costs, staff training, taxation, etc.

(2) Capital figures may not be comparable because of differences in policy of buying or leasing some assets, capitalising or writing off certain types of expenditure, the treatment of goodwill and intangibles (e.g. patents) etc.

(3) Return on capital is probably not suitable for businesses selling the services of skilled staff (e.g. management consultants, advertising agents, accountants, valuers, stockbrokers) who do not appear in the balance sheet as assets.

(4) The return on capital ratio should always be looked at for a number of years and primarily, but not exclusively, compared with companies in the same industry (and therefore experiencing a similar economic environment).

(5) Profit will not include capital appreciations until realised, although these will have increased the size of the capital figure and thus depressed the return on capital ratio.

(6) As is discussed later (page 67 below) property values may have been reduced before incorporation in the accounts because of a lack of profitability. Any return on capital that is then calculated on such a reduced valuation will merely reflect (a) the directors' estimate of an adequate level of profitability and (b) their ability to achieve their own expectations.

Asset backing

If a company is earning a low return on capital or running at a loss, then the investor and the analyst will become increasingly interested in the company's asset backing as measured by the ratio of net assets per share. This is a ratio which analysts use sparingly and with caution, because often values in the balance sheet for property and plant are out of date and too low and, secondly, it is well known that if a company goes into liquidation it is rare for its non property assets to be sold at anything like their balance sheet figure — they usually fetch far less. Moreover properties sold in a liquidation are often disposed of on a different basis of valuation from that used in the balance sheet e.g. 'alternative use value' or 'forced sale value' as opposed to 'existing use value'.

The long-term lender

The long-term lender to a company is interested in an up-to-date value of the company's property as an indication of the security for his lending. Few, if any, lenders will want the company to sell its property in order to repay the loan. They would prefer the loan interest and capital repayments to be made out of profits and if necessary fresh borrowing. Nevertheless the prudent lender would not want to find the value of his security to have dropped significantly if the need to use it should arise.

The finance director

The finance director of a company may want an up-to-date valuation of the company's property in order to increase the size of the company's borrowing base, and/or to calculate a more realistic rate of return on capital for management control purposes, and/or to improve the company's asset value per share as a partial protection against unwelcome takeover bids.

Profit and depreciation

Many users of accounts are most interested in the size of a company's profit, and one of the factors in arriving at profit will be the deduction for depreciation of property. The equity investor will look at profit to see how large his dividend could be, the lender will look at profit to see how safe his interest payments are (how many times they are covered by pre-interest profits). The employee may look at profits to see how large a wage rise the company can 'afford'. The taxman uses the profit figure as a basis for his demands, (although he ignores the company's own figure for depreciation and substitutes his own) and the company's suppliers and customers might use the size of profit in seeking respectively a price increase or reduction.

II

The accountants' and auditors' approach

4 Company accounts: law, recommendations and practice

A company's annual report and accounts is the vehicle by means of which the directors of a company report and account to the owners of the company on their stewardship for the past year. It is rare, except among smaller companies, for the annual accounts to be used by management to help them manage the business. For that they will (or should) have management accounts prepared in more detail, more frequently and more quickly.

A limited company's accounts must be audited, but it is important to note that the auditor's report only covers the accounts and not, for example, the directors' report and chairman's statement which often together occupy the major part of the company's 'annual report' (see Diagram 1).

The content of published accounts is governed partly by law, partly by the recommendations and Statements of Standard Accounting Practice (SSAPs) of the professional bodies concerned (The Accounting Standards Committee, The Institute of Chartered Accountants in England and Wales, and the Royal Institution of Chartered Surveyors), and partly by what is regarded as good practice. In addition listed companies are required to make additional disclosure in their published accounts, as a result of the Stock Exchange listing agreement, but none of this additional disclosure relates to property values. However, the Stock Exchange does require disclosure about property values in a prospectus (see below).

The discussion which follows is limited to disclosure relating to property values and depreciation.

Company Law
The Companies Act 1948 as amended by the Companies Act 1967

Diagram 1

The relationship between the valuer, accountant, directors, chairman, auditors and users of the annual report

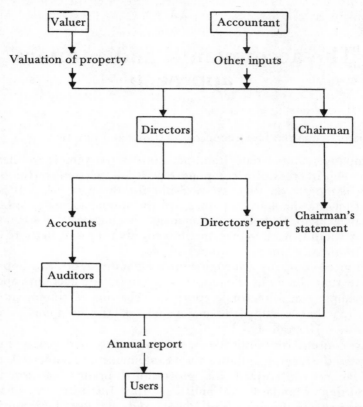

requires (Schedule 2, 11(6A)) the accounts to state the method by which the amount included in the balance sheet for property has been arrived at. This may be either cost, or valuation, or a mixture of both, less accumulated depreciation (if any — but see the reference to SSAP 12 below). The notes to the accounts must show (a) the years of valuation (if known) and (b) the values placed on the property in each separate year of valuation. If the valuation took place during the year the name of the valuer or his qualifications must be shown, and the bases of valuation used must be stated.

Interests in land must be analysed between freehold, long leaseholds (over 50 years unexpired) and short leaseholds (Schedule 2,

10

11(6C)). The Companies Act 1967 (Section 16 (1) (a)) also states that the directors' report shall "if significant changes in the fixed assets of the company or of any of its subsidiaries have occurred in that year, contain particulars of the changes, and, if, in the case of such of those assets as consist in interests in land the market value thereof (as at the end of that year) differs substantially from the amount at which they are included in the balance sheet and the difference is, in the opinion of the directors of such significance as to require the attention of members of the company or of holders of debentures thereof should be drawn thereto, indicate the difference with such degree of precision as is practicable".

It will be noted that not only has the market value to differ substantially from the figure in the balance sheet, but that, in the opinion of the directors, the difference is sufficiently significant for it to be drawn to the attention of the shareholders or debenture holders. (For a discussion of this section of the Companies Act see Section 15 below.)

Stock Exchange requirements

The Stock Exchange requirements for property valuations in a prospectus are shown in Appendix 6. In summary the relevant requirements are:

(a) Details of each property should include:
  (i) Address
  (ii) Description, age and tenure
  (iii) Terms of tenants' leases and underleases
  (iv) Estimated net annual current rental before taxation
  (v) Present capital value in existing state
(b) If the properties held are too numerous to enable all such particulars to be given without undue length, the Stock Exchange Department should be consulted. In some cases suitable condensed details may be acceptable. In other cases it may be acceptable to have a detailed valuation report available for inspection, and a summarised valuation report included in the prospectus.
(c) The valuation report must state whether the valuation is based on open market value, or, if necessary, depreciated replacement cost subject to adequate profitability.

(d) Property should be classified as follows:
   (i) Held as investments
   (ii) Being developed
   (iii) Held for development in the future
   (iv) Held for disposal
   (v) Owner-occupied;
and
   (i) Freehold
   (ii) Leasehold

Accountants' guidance
The Institute of Chartered Accountants in England and Wales issued guidance on the subject to its members in February 1974 in Statement S20 (reproduced in full in Appendix 1). This recommends:

(a) the basis of any valuation should be clearly stated
(b) the 'going concern' basis is unsuitable
(c) the acceptable bases, when and how often they should be used are set out in Guidance Notes issued by the Royal Institution of Chartered Surveyors (R.I.C.S) and prepared by a joint working party of chartered accountants and surveyors.

Surveyors' guidance
The R.I.C.S. Guidance Notes (A2) are reproduced in full in Appendix 2. They state, in summary:

(a) An open market valuation may be on an existing use or alternative use basis.
(b) Open market value may be higher or lower than depreciated replacement cost (i.e. the current cost of acquiring the site, and erecting the premises less a deduction to allow for their present condition).
(c) Property valuations for use in accounts or directors' reports should be on the basis of open market value, except in special cases where a property is rarely, if ever, sold except as part of the business (e.g. an oil refinery), when depreciated replacement cost may be used.
(d) Open market existing use valuations or depreciated replacement cost are to be used for valuing operational properties in owner occupation and are suitable for accounts drawn up on a going concern basis. Alternative use valuations are suitable only for the directors' report, but this may contain existing use valuations as well, or instead.

12

(e) Where potential changes to the value of a company's property are material, valuations should be carried out every three to five years.

Statements of Standard Accounting Practice
The two Statements of Standard Accounting Practice (SSAP) which are relevant to this book are numbers 2 and 12 relating to Accounting Policies and Depreciation respectively. They are reproduced in full in Appendices 3 and 4. The key points they make are:

(a) Companies should disclose their accounting policies.
(b) All accounts should be based on four fundamental concepts:
    (i) consistency
    (ii) going concern
    (iii) accruals
    (iv) prudence
(c) The relevance of the consistency concept to property valuation is that under it the method and bases of valuation should be the same every year and not be changed because, for example, the company has done well or badly in one particular year.
(d) The going concern concept is particularly important for property valuations because it assumes that the business will continue and it will not be necessary to effect a forced sale of the property in the near future.
(e) The accruals concept says that a company should match income and expenditure. This means that, for example, the cost of property is spread over its useful life, and not written off more rapidly than that, nor, only when the directors consider there are enough profits to do so.
(f) The prudence concept has been described as 'not counting your chickens before they are hatched'. Revenue and profits are not anticipated but only included when realised. Unrealised profits (e.g. surplus on revaluation of property) are taken to reserve and not shown in the profit and loss account until they are realised. On the other hand provision is made for all known liabilities (expenses and losses).
(g) All non-investment property should be depreciated over its useful life. Depreciation is defined as a measure of wearing out, consumption or other loss of value whether arising from use, the passage of time, or obsolescence through technological or market changes. This is particularly relevant to property which may become obsolete long before its physical life is over.

13

A fundamental accounting convention that is often misunderstood by non accountants is that the balance sheet is not intended to be a valuation statement. It is a statement of costs which have been incurred but not yet written off through the profit and loss account. This convention — part of the historical cost convention — has been breached by permitting, but not requiring, revaluations of property and plant.

There are two ways in which an asset may be written off through the profit and loss account. The normal way is to charge a suitable part of the cost of the asset to each year's profit and loss account during the economic life of the asset, and thus match the cost of the asset to the revenue earned by its employment. Sometimes, however, it becomes apparent that future revenue will not be adequate to cover the balance of the cost of the asset not yet written off. In that situation, that part of the balance of the cost of the asset not covered by estimated future revenue would be written off immediately.

Current cost accounting

Current cost accounting requires regular revaluations of most assets but it is being introduced gradually and mainly as a supplement to the historical cost accounts of listed and the largest non-listed companies.

The latest pronouncement on the subject of current cost accounting in the U.K. is SSAP 16 and the accompanying Guidance Notes published by the Accounting Standards Committee on 31st March 1980.

Under SSAP 16 land and buildings should be shown in the current cost balance sheet at their 'value to the business'. This is defined as:

(a) the net current replacement cost;
   or, if a permanent diminution in the value of the asset to below net replacement cost has been recognised,
(b) its recoverable amount.

The recoverable amount is the greater of the net realisable value of the asset and, where applicable, the amount recoverable from its further use.

A 'depreciation adjustment' should be charged in the current cost profit and loss account equal to the difference between the value to the business of the fixed assets consumed in the period and depreciation calculated on the historical cost basis.

Surpluses (or deficits) on revaluation should be transferred to (or from) current cost reserves in the current cost balance sheet, but any amount required to reduce assets from net current replacement cost to recoverable amount should be charged to the profit and loss account.

The guidance notes on SSAP 16 (which are not mandatory) divide the treatment of land and buildings into five categories:

(a) owner-occupied – specialised buildings
(b) owner-occupied – non-specialised buildings
(c) owner-occupied – non-specialised (including trading potential)
(d) investment properties
(e) surplus properties

Specialised buildings, because of their location or arrangement, the form of their construction, or perhaps their size, are rarely sold except by way of sale of the business in which they are used. Typically many industrial buildings on works' sites come into this category. The current cost of such buildings should be evaluated on the same principles as plant and machinery (see below). The underlying land should be valued on the basis applying to non-specialised buildings unless it is immaterial in relation to the total assets of the business.

However, certain kinds of buildings, such as hotels, petrol filling stations, cinemas, public houses, are normally valued and recorded in the historical cost accounts on a basis which includes inherent trading potential* (also commonly referred to as 'goodwill which runs with the property'). They are commonly bought and sold as continuing businesses. Accordingly, they should be treated as non-specialised buildings because the written down replacement cost basis which is used for specialised buildings cannot be applied to the goodwill element.

Non-specialised buildings, such as the majority of offices, shops and general purpose industrial units should be valued at their open market value for existing use plus acquisition costs.

Investment properties should be valued at their open market value plus acquisition costs (if these are material and have been capitalised in the historical cost accounts).

Surplus property should be valued at open market value less costs of disposal.

---

* Reference to the Background Paper No. 7 prepared by the R.I.C.S. may also be of assistance in the valuation of such properties.

Adaptation costs should be treated like plant and machinery and the basic property separately valued.

Buildings under construction should be valued as follows:

(a) specialised — same method as for plant
(b) non-specialised — at the *lower* of
    (i) indexed cost
    (ii) estimated completed open market value *less* estimated cost to complete, both at current prices

Specialised property and adaptation costs should be valued in the same way as plant and machinery. This means calculating the gross replacement cost and depreciating it by reference to the proportion of its total working life that has expired. The most convenient way of calculating gross replacement cost will be by indexing historical cost but if there has been substantial technological change, or if the price movement of the asset is known to have deviated significantly from the movement of the index, or if the original cost was affected by unusual circumstances, then the gross replacement cost should be based on expert opinion of the cost of an asset having the same service potential.

Table 2	
Valuation of property under CCA	
Category	*Basis of valuation*

Owner occupied
  specialised
    buildings
    land
	
	DRC
	OMV for existing use

non-specialised	OMV for existing use + acquisition costs
non-specialised (including trading potential)	OMV for existing use including trading potential which runs with the property
Investment	OMV + acquisition costs
Surplus	OMV — disposal costs

Adapted property
  basic property
  adaptation costs
	
	Market value*
	DRC

* As for non-specialised above

16

The auditor's responsibilities

The auditor has to report that the company's accounts give a 'true and fair view'. The auditor arrives at his opinion by examining evidence about the company's activities and financial position. When it comes to property he will need to satisfy himself that the company owns the property, and that the directors' reasons for their estimate of its remaining useful life are acceptable — bearing in mind its age and condition. If it has been revalued he should study the valuer's report, and one of the questions explored in this book is what may he find in it, and how should he react to its contents.

An auditor is entitled to ask the directors and employees of the company for "such information and explanation as he thinks necessary for the performance of his audit". If he fails to get the information he *must* qualify his report (CA 1967 ss14(5) and (6)). An internal valuer is an employee and is therefore legally obliged to provide the auditor with information. An external valuer is not an employee and is not therefore legally obliged to provide the auditor with any more information than in his (the valuer's) report. However the R.I.C.S. say "It is probably in the valuer's own interest that the auditors should, if they so wish, inspect the whole of his file, in that a negligent act or incorrect information might be ascertained before damage is caused; failure to produce a file could conceivably lend colour to more serious allegations where there was any subsequent action alleging something beyond negligence"* and that "It is the view of the Assets Valuations Standards Committee of the R.I.C.S. that members should be prepared to co-operate reasonably and responsibly if they are approached by auditors".

The auditor should check that the information supplied to the valuer by the directors is not misleading either by commission or omission. It must be remembered that the auditor has more power to insist on answers to questions than the valuer has.

The auditor is entitled to rely on the valuer's valuation expertise but should check the information supplied to him, the nature of his instructions and should consider to what extent it is necessary for parts of the report to be included in the accounts in order to give a 'true and fair view'.

Company practice — Survey of Published Accounts

Despite the legislation and recommendations of professional bodies, the proportion of published accounts which provide users with up-to-

* RICS Guidance Note G2

Table 3

Revaluation of fixed assets

	Number of companies			
	Property		*Other fixed assets*	
	1977-78	*1976-77*	*1977-78*	*1976-77*
Most recent major revaluation shown in:				
year of account	34	26	4	2
previous 4 years	94	120	8	9
5 to 9 years earlier . . .	35	18	—	3
10 or more years earlier	13	13	1	2
	176	177	13	16
Some fixed assets at a valuation, but not a large portion	54	65	53	74
No material revaluation shown	70	58	234	210
	300	300	300	300
Proportion of total book amount based on valuations, not necessarily recent:				
76% to 100%	83	86	1	1
51 to 75%	55	56	2	5
26 to 50%	42	42	10	9
	180	184	13	15
up to 25%	50	57	53	74
	230	241	66	89
No material amount shown at a valuation . .	70	59	234	211
	300	300	300	300

date property values is small. Tables 3, 4 and 5 are reproduced, with permission, from the *Survey of Published Accounts 1978* published by The Institute of Chartered Accountants in England and Wales.

These tables show that, out of the top 300 companies in the U.K.,

(a) just over half (176 out of 300) have had a major property revaluation, but

(b) just over 40% (128 out of 300) have had a major property revaluation in the last four years.

Table 4

Statements as to market value of property

	Number of companies		
	1977-78	*1976-77*	*1975-76*
Statement provided:			
assessment of value mainly by:			
directors	131	108	112
professional valuers	36	69	61
	167	177	173
no assessment of value	5	12	11
	172	189	184
No statement provided	128	111	116
	300	300	300

Table 5

Degree of precision in assessment of value of property

	Number of companies	
	1977-78	*1976-77*
Statement provided:		
Precise figures	21	36
Approximations (Note 1)	35	35
	56	71
Qualitative assessment (Note 2)	111	106
	167	177
No statement or no assessment of value	133	123
	300	300

Notes:
1. Approximations include cases where there has been either a rough estimate of current market value or where directors are of the opinion that a precise estimate made, say, a year ago has not altered materially.
2. Qualitative assessments incorporate such phrases as "market value exceeds book value" or "market value is less than book value".

(c) just over half (167 out of 300) provide a statement of current value, but

(d) most of these (131) are based on directors' assessments and only 36 were provided by professional valuers,

(e) of the statements provided, two thirds are described as qualitative and were not quantified.

What is not immediately apparent from the Tables is that in many instances properties have been revalued on a piecemeal basis at various dates in past years, and the balance sheet total is made up of

Table 6		
Location of Valuation		
	No.	%
Valuation:		
In accounts only	26	28
In directors' report only	21	22
Both	39	41
Statement of reason why no valuation was given	1	2
No reference to valuation	7	7
	94	100

the sum of these valuations together with other properties shown at cost and any additional expenses incurred since the last revaluation.

It seems fair to assume that a lower proportion of firms smaller than the top 300 would provide even this information.

There would appear to be a significant deficiency in the provision of relevant information to the users of accounts in this area.

Table 7	
Number of different years' valuations used in the accounts	
No. of different years of valuations used	*No. of Companies*
1	1
2	16
3	13
4	10
5	9
6	2
7	4
8	3
9	2
10	1
11	1
Insufficient detail given in the accounts	3
	65

Table 8

Proportion of valuation and cost in different years of valuation

Valuation	0-10 %	11-20 %	21-30 %	31-40 %	41-50 %	51-60 %	61-70 %	71-80 %	81-90 %	91-100 %
Year of Account	6	3	2	1		2	2			4
Previous year	8		4		1	1	1		1	1
2 years ago	11	2		2		2	1	1	2	
3 years ago	16	3		1		1		1	2	
4 years ago	8	4	1	2	1	1	2	2		
5 years ago	11	2	2		1			1		
6-10 years ago	13	4			2					
11-15 years ago	13	3	3		1	1		1		
16-20 years ago	5									
21-30 years ago	5									
Cost	8	6	10	7	5	9	4	6	2	5
	104	27	22	13	11	17	10	12	7	10

Company practice — our own research
Whilst the information from the *Survey of Published Accounts* is interesting and valuable, it was considered that it did not go into sufficient depth for the purposes of this book. It was therefore decided to conduct our own analysis. We selected a random sample of 94 out of the 300 accounts included in the Institute's survey and our findings are set out below.

93% of the companies included a valuation of their property in their annual report (28% in the accounts; 22% in the directors' report; 41% in both) — see Table 6.

This rosy picture is somewhat dimmed by the fact that rarely has property all been valued at the same date (see Table 7). Whilst two different years is the most common number of years of valuation, 3, 4 and 5 years are almost as common, and some companies have used as many as 9, 10 or 11 different years' valuations.

The data in Table 7 is further expanded in Table 8. This shows the proportion of cost and valuation, and the age of the valuation, for those companies which showed a valuation in their accounts. The figures show the number of occasions each combination occurred,

	No.	%
Table 9		
Valuations in the directors' report		
Qualitative:		
by directors		
excess of book value	15	25
equal to/or not less than book value	11	19
based on professional valuation		
excess of book value	2	3
equal to book value	3	5
Quantitative:		
by directors		
£ excess reflected in the accounts*	3	5
based on professional valuation		
£ excess not reflected in the accounts	10	17
£ excess reflected in the accounts*	8	13
No detailed information (unable to assess)	8	13
	60	100

* Only 11 companies above actually reflect the information contained in the directors' report in the accounts. Generally it was found that more up-to-date information was contained in the directors' report. In no instance was the information found to be in conflict with that in the accounts.

e.g. the first figure in the first column shows that 6 companies had revalued between 0 and 10% of their property in the year of account. The ideal would be a high proportion of property valued recently.

Table 8 shows that only four companies had valued between 91% and 100% of their property in the year of the accounts. Only one company had revalued 100% of its property. 30 (48%) companies had valued at least 50% of their property (in one valuation) (12 (19%) in year of account or previous, 18 (29%) at least two years prior to the year of account). 26 (41%) companies showed at least 50% of their property at cost. The remaining 8 companies would have had more than one valuation covering more than 50% of their property.

Many companies have had minor valuations covering only a small percentage of property. This would suggest that these were made for a particular reason and not as a result of a general decision to revalue property.

Table 9 shows, for the 60 companies which had a valuation in the directors' report (see Table 6), whether the information was (a) qualitative or quantitative (b) based on the directors' valuation or a professional one, and (c) incorporated in the accounts or not. Only 30% were quantified and based on a professional valuation; 25% were

(text continues at foot of page 27)

Table 10
Names and qualifications of valuers

	Accounts		Directors' Report	
	No.	%	No.	%
Neither name nor qualification	34	52		
Valuers/professionally qualified valuers				
named	4	6		
not named	1	2		
Chartered Surveyors				
named	5	8	6	10
not named	4	6	1	2
Professional valuations				
named	1	2	1	2
not named	10	15	4	6
Independent valuations				
named			1	2
not named	3	4	1	2
Directors/company staff	2	3	44	73
Name stated — no qualifications	1	2	2	3
	65	100	60	100

23

Table 11

Basis of valuation

	Accounts No.	%	Directors' Report No.	%
No basis mentioned	42	64	43	70
Open market value and variations				
'Open market value/basis'	3	4	3	5
'Sums that might reasonably have been obtained on sales in the open market with vacant possession of the parts then occupied by the group'	—	—	1	2
'Vacant possession basis'	2	3	1	2
'Open market value with vacant possession'	1	2	1	2
	6	9	6	11
Open market value for existing use and variations				
'Existing use'	2	3	6	10
'Present use, as between willing buyer and willing seller with no account of any potential development value'	1	2	—	—
'Open market for existing use'	3	4	2	3
'Market value with vacant possession and on the basis of existing permitted planning use'	1	2	—	—
	7	11	8	13
Replacement cost/inflation				
'Current replacement cost'	1	2	—	—
'Depreciated replacement cost'	—	—	1	2
'In accordance with local inflation accounting regulations'	1	2	—	—
'N.Z. current official government valuation'	1	2	—	—
	3	6	1	2

Continued

24

Table 11 – *Continued*

Going concern basis		2	3	–	–
Mixed bases					
'Existing use and alternative use'	A*	3	4	1	2
'Open market value and depreciated replacement cost'	B*	–	–	1	2
'Existing use or open market value'	C*	1	2	–	–
'Existing use, for sale, and open market value or existing use'	D*	1	1	–	–
		5	7	2	4
		65	100	60	100

*Notes to Table 11: Extracts from Company Accounts

(A) Existing use and alternative use

British Printing Corporation Ltd   Note to Accounts
The Group's industrial and commercial freehold and leasehold properties were revalued as at 1st January 1977 by Leopold Farmer and Sons, Surveyors and Valuers, on both an 'existing use' basis and an 'alternative use' basis. The directors have adopted the 'existing use' valuations for the majority of properties and 'alternative use' values for the remainder except for some other properties where a lower valuation has been used. The analysis of the values remaining at 31st December 1977 is as follows:

	Value on existing use £'000	Value adopted £'000
Properties valued on an 'existing use' basis	11,815	11,815
Properties valued on an alternative use basis	10,668	8,387
Properties at directors' valuation but below the 'alternative use' basis	430	206
	22,913	20,408
In addition, and at the same date, BPC's house properties were revalued by local valuers on an 'existing use' basis assuming vacant possession. These values are reflected in the accounts	1,822	1,822
	24,735	22,230
Subsequent additions at cost		1,039
		£23,269

25

Bridon Ltd   Note to Accounts
At 31st December 1977 a professional valuation was carried out and the results incorporated into the Group accounts in respect of all land and buildings previously stated in the accounts at a cost or valuation considered to be significantly different from the current market values. Properties have been valued on an existing use basis with the exception of £835,000 properties in the United Kingdom which have been valued on an alternative use basis. Of the £18,546,000 Freehold and Leasehold properties at the valuation at 31st December 1977, £14,880,000 is in the United Kingdom and was valued by Maynard and Co., Chartered Surveyors, and £3,666,000 is overseas and was valued by locally qualified valuers.

Cadbury Schweppes Ltd   Notes to Accounts
The freehold and leasehold properties of the Group were revalued during the year. The valuations were carried out as at 30th September 1977 and were incorporated in the accounts at 31st December 1977.

Properties with a book value of £122.3m were revalued at £123.9m as below:

	£m
Professionally valued	
Existing use valuation	88.2
Alternative use valuation	12.6
Valued by directors	
Locally accepted indices	9.9
Alternative use valuation	5.2
Existing use valuation	8.0
	123.9

The valuers of the major properties held by Cadbury Schweppes Limited and of the properties of the principal subsidiary companies were:

Cadbury Schweppes Ltd	Grimley and Sons
	Henry Butcher and Co.
	Strutt and Parker
Subsidiaries:	
C.S. Foods Ltd	Grimley and Sons
	Henry Butcher and Co.
C.S. Australia Ltd	Richard Ellis
C.S. (South Africa) Ltd	Dunlop Heywood
Cadbury Ireland Ltd	Thornton and Partners

Cadbury Schweppes Ltd   Directors' Report
The freehold and leasehold properties of the Group were revalued as at 30th September 1977 and valuations incorporated into the accounts at 31st December 1977. The properties were professionally valued except in cases where cost or other circumstances justified a valuation by the Directors.

The valuation was carried out on an existing use basis except in cases where a change of use of property is contemplated when the alternative use basis of valuation has been adopted.

26

(B) Open market value and depreciated replacement cost

W. Collins and Sons Ltd   Directors' Report
Independent valuations of the Group's properties were carried out during 1977.
The valuations are in excess of book values by £3,144,000.

	Valuation	Book value	Excess
	£'000	£'000	£'000
Freehold property valued at open market value	2,711	1,596	1,115
Freehold property valued at depreciated replacement cost	15,796	13,911	1,885
Leasehold property	230	86	144
	18,737	15,593	3,144
Leasehold property not valued		24	
Buildings in course of construction		1,069	
		16,686	

(C) Existing use or open market value

Coral Leisure Ltd   Notes to Accounts
All valuations were made by independent professional valuers on the basis of an
existing use or open market value of the relevant properties.

(D) Existing use, for sale, and open market value or existing use

Delta Metal Co. Ltd

Accounting Policy:
'Freehold and leasehold property in the U.K. is mainly revalued on an existing
use basis, each property being valued once in three years.
   'Overseas properties are revalued regularly mainly on an existing use or open
market basis, the period between valuations varies depending on local conditions.'

Note to Accounts:
'The revaluations which were made in 1977 comprise: U.K. £15.05m on an
existing use basis and £1.23m on a for sale basis . . . . . . and overseas mainly on an
open market or existing use basis.'

(text continued from page 23)

based on a directors' valuation and stated no more than that their
valuation was in excess of book value.
   Table 10 shows what information was given about the names and/
or qualifications of the valuers (see page 10 above). 34 (52%) gave
neither the name nor the qualification of the valuers in the accounts.
A very high proportion (73%) of the valuations in the directors'
report were by the directors or company staff but it was not apparent
whether or not they were professionally qualified.
   It would appear from this table that users are not being provided

with all the information that they need. There is certainly scope for an improvement in company practice in this area.

Table 11 shows what information was given about the basis of the valuation(s) used in the accounts and/or directors' reports. (The notes to Table 11 are on pages 25 to 27.)

Forty-three companies in their accounts and 43 in the directors' report did not give the basis of the valuation. We have already seen how important it is for the user to have this information. Directors should be encouraged to provide it more frequently than at present.

The remaining companies used a wide range of descriptions which suggest that the revaluations may well not be comparable. Even when we have grouped them into similar descriptions we are left with at least five groups. It would appear that there is scope for greater uniformity of description of valuations by valuers and directors and it is to be hoped that the relevant professional bodies will encourage this.

One of the major possible reasons why a company might be left with less cash than the book amount or any valuation of its property from any sale of it, may be the necessity to pay tax on the so called capital gain. 55% of the companies made no mention of this pitfall; 29% mentioned it but did not quantify it; and 16% had made a provision for this contingent liability (see Table 12 and also Section 16 below).

	No.	%
No mention made	52	55
Provision made for tax on surplus on sale of assets	15	16
Stated that no provision has been made	27	29
	94	100

Table 12

Treatment of Potential Taxation

5 Depreciation

The different meanings of depreciation

Depreciation is inextricably linked with valuation. In some cases the valuation is used as a basis to calculate depreciation; in other cases depreciation is used to arrive at a 'valuation' e.g. a depreciated replacement cost valuation.

Part of the problem is that the one word 'depreciation' is used to

28

cover a relatively wide range of meanings, both when used by 'experts', such as accountants and surveyors, and when used by directors, investors, etc., as will be seen later in this Section. For example:

(a) Depreciation is the process of allocating the cost of an asset over its useful life.

(b) Depreciation is the process of allocating a current value of an asset over its remaining useful life.

(c) Depreciation is the process of reducing original cost or a previous valuation to a current value.

(d) Depreciation is the mechanism by means of which funds are retained to finance the replacement of an asset when necessary.

Other aspects of the problem are:

(1) whether or not values drop evenly over the life of an asset

(2) whether depreciation of an asset should match any drop in value

(3) should depreciation be a function of time or use, or both?

(4) should depreciation relate to physical life or economic life, i.e. the problem of obsolescence?

(5) should depreciation be revised in the light of the adequacy of maintenance and repairs?

(6) is depreciation necessary if the value of the property is rising?

Official definitions

SSAP12 has defined depreciation as "the measure of wearing out, consumption, or other loss of value of a fixed asset whether arising from use, effluxion of time or obsolescence through technology and market changes". According to SSAP12 provision for depreciation should be made by allocating the cost (or revalued amounts) as fairly as possible to the periods expected to benefit from the use of the asset. This definition is similar to definitions (a) and (b) above.

SSAP 16, on the other hand, describes depreciation as "the value to the business of the fixed assets consumed during the period". The guidance notes elaborate this definition. As far as property is concerned depreciation is to be calculated on the 'building' element in the valuation of the property (Guidance Notes on SSAP 16: Current Cost Accounting, paragraph 34). Depreciation will depend not only on estimated current replacement costs but on the estimated length of asset lives. The guidance notes (paragraph 12) set out a general principle that changes in net current cost book value due to:

(a) price changes are taken to current cost reserves.

(b) other reasons (e.g. changes in estimated life) are taken to profit and loss account.

This appears to be an elaboration of definition (c) above.

The guidance notes on ED 24 said that "the current cost depreciation charge is normally sufficient . . . . . to make adequate provision in the accounts for the current replacement cost of the asset at the end of its life" (Guidance Notes on ED 24, paragraph 36)*. This is similar to definition (d) above.

Shareholders' understanding of depreciation

Lee and Tweedie† found, in a survey of 301 private shareholders in a very large public company, that their understanding of the term depreciation was as follows:

		%	Definition
(a)	**Reasonable Understanding**		
	Amount written off fixed assets over time or life of assets concerned	13	a or b
	Loss in value of fixed assets, wear and tear on fixed assets	13	c
		26	
(b)	**Vague Understanding**		
	Amount written off assets	18	a or b
	Loss in value of assets, wear and tear on assets.	27	c
	Answers suggesting depreciation is a means of replacing fixed assets	7	d
	Other vague answers	4	
		56	
(c)	**No Understanding**	18	
		100	

This suggests that:

31% were using definitions (a) or (b)

40% were using definition (c) and 7% were using definition (d)

* The whole of paragraph 36 reads: "The current cost depreciation charge is normally sufficient, taken together with the other CCA adjustments, to make adequate provision in the accounts for the current replacement cost of the asset at the end of its life. Although the total of the depreciation charges made against profits will have been less than the replacement cost by the amount of the backlog depreciation, the assets representing the accumulated depreciation will probably have been the subject of other CCA adjustments. However, the actual provision of funds for purchasing new fixed assets remains a matter for financial management". The wording of the corresponding paragraph in the SSAP 16 Guidance Notes (Paragraph 52) is less clear, but the intention seems to be the same.

† *The Private Shareholder and the Corporate Report,* Institute of Chartered Accountants in England and Wales, 1977, p. 163.

Depreciation and valuation

If depreciation is regarded as a charge for the use of an asset, and, if the value of the asset is increasing, then it does not reduce the need to charge for its use. On the contrary, it suggests the desirability of increasing the charge! The increase in value should be reported separately from the charge for depreciation. Such an increase may of course merely reflect, in whole or in part, the effect of inflation. Moreover the increase will not be 'realised' until either the asset is sold or its increased value is charged, as depreciation, to the profit and loss account.

Depreciation, repairs and refurbishment

It is possible to imagine a situation where the amount spent on repairs is such that there is no physical depreciation of the buildings during the year and it might then be argued that the cost of using the buildings was the amount spent on repairs and that there was no need to provide depreciation as well. This, however, ignores the probability that the building may still be in the process of becoming obsolete even if it is not physically deteriorating and that depreciation should still be provided albeit at a lower rate than if the repairs had not been carried out.

A building may of course be substantially refurbished and thus given an extension to its economic life. If the refurbishment costs were charged to the profit and loss account it might be argued that there was no need to provide depreciation as well. It would be more equitable as between one period and another however to add the refurbishment costs to the original cost, or pre-refurbishment valuation, and then depreciate the total over the new, extended life, and thus spread the cost over the period of benefit, rather than unfairly penalise the results of the year in which the refurbishment took place.

Apportionment of valuation for depreciation purposes

As normally it is the buildings which wear out, become obsolete, or depreciate, whilst the land on which they are constructed does not*, it is usual for accountants to provide depreciation on buildings but not on land. Such a policy however requires the cost or value of the property to be divided between buildings and land and this sometimes causes problems. If the property has been valued by arriving at separate figures for buildings and land then there will be no problem

* Land does of course depreciate in such cases as planning consents for a limited period of time, and quarries, etc.

in finding a figure for buildings upon which to base depreciation, unless the valuation has been reduced by the directors before inclusion in the balance sheet on the grounds of inadequate profitability. In such cases there might be a problem as to how best to allocate this reduction to land and buildings but it is suggested that the reduction should be applied wholly to the 'building' element as the 'land' is normally unaffected by the profitability of the business being conducted on it.

Where however the property has been valued at open market value it is necessary to apportion this between 'buildings' and 'land' in order to have a basis for the depreciation of buildings. The R.I.C.S. has given guidance to its members on this subject as follows (Guidance Note J1):

> Where the property has been acquired and is carried in the balance sheet at cost or has been the subject of a past or present open market valuation which has been incorporated in the balance sheet, it is necessary for the valuer to ascertain the value applicable to the buildings and the value of the land by an apportionment of cost or valuation as between buildings and land. The building element will be the 'depreciable amount' and the land element will be the 'residual amount' (termed residual value in SSAP 12).
>
> The apportionment may be arrived at in one of two ways:
>
> (a) By deducting from the cost or valuation of the asset the value of the land for its existing use at the relevant date. In many instances there will be ample evidence of land values upon which a notional apportionment can be made. However, for many central urban properties there may be little or no evidence of land values and in such cases greater reliance will have to be placed on method (b) below.
>
> (b) By making an assessment of the net replacement cost of the buildings at the relevant date. This figure will be derived from gross replacement cost which will be the actual cost of the buildings or if this is not known, the estimated cost. The gross replacement cost is then reduced to the written-down or net replacement cost to reflect the value of the asset to the business.
>
> In any particular case it should be possible for the valuer to arrive at a depreciable amount, which fairly reflects that part of the open market value or cost of the whole property at the time it was acquired or valued, which can be expressed as the value to the business at that time of the buildings on the land.
>
> When providing figures for the purposes of depreciation the valuer should emphasise in the report that the resultant figures, i.e. the depreciable amount and the residual amount, are informal apportionments and that the individual figures do not represent the open market value of the building and land elements.

This is no doubt very practical advice, but it is easy to imagine that methods (a) and (b) above could give materially different results.

For example:

In 1977 a freehold factory consisted of two buildings, one of 20,000 sq. ft. built in 1967, and the other of 15,000 sq. ft. built in 1952 and was on a site of 1½ acres. Rental values in the area were £1.50 per sq. ft., investment yields were 10%, land in the area sold at £70,000 per acre and building costs were £20 per sq. ft. This gave a valuation of £525,000 (20,000 sq. ft. + 15,000 sq. ft. = 35,000 sq. ft. x £1.50 per sq. ft. x 100% ÷ 10%). Both buildings were assumed to have total lives of 60 years from new.

Using method (a)
Value of property	£525,000
Less value of land (1.5 acres x £70,000)	£105,000
Depreciable Amount	£420,000

Using method (b)

Building no. 1 (built 1967 therefore age = 10 years)

Gross replacement cost

20,000 sq. ft. x £20 per sq. ft. = £400,000

Net replacement cost

$$\frac{60 \text{ years} - 10 \text{ years}}{60 \text{ years}} \text{ x £400,000} = £333,333$$

Building no. 2 (built 1952 therefore age = 25 years)

Gross replacement cost

15,000 sq. ft. x £20 per sq. ft. = £300,000

Net replacement cost

$$\frac{60 \text{ years} - 25 \text{ years}}{60 \text{ years}} \text{ x £300,000} = £175,000$$

Depreciable amount
Building no. 1	£333,333
Building no. 2	£175,000
	£508,333

Summary
Depreciable amount method (a)	£420,000
Depreciable amount method (b)	£508,000
A difference of	£ 88,000
	or 21% of (a)

Methods (a) and (b) appear to represent different philosophies of depreciation. The argument for method (a) is that if the value of the land is taken away from the value of the property then what is left is the wasting or depreciating amount because, normally, the value of the land does not depreciate. Method (a) appears to be based on concept (b) of depreciation (page 29 above).

The argument for method (b) is that the company should set aside enough money out of revenue to replace its buildings when they reach the end of their economic life. Method (b) appears to be more consistent therefore with depreciation concept (d).

It would be desirable for the R.I.C.S. and A.S.C.:

(a) to suggest that, if the amount is material, then the fact of such an apportionment and the method used should be disclosed in the notes to the accounts.

(b) to indicate a preference for either method (a) or method (b) above.

(c) to consider the advantages and disadvantages of not requiring a split of a property valuation into land and buildings elements but to calculate depreciation on the total value of the property where depreciation so calculated would not have a material effect on the profit figure (see also Section 8 below).

It is possible for the depreciated replacement cost to exceed the open market value. In this case depreciation would be calculated only on the open market value on the grounds that one should not write off more than is in the balance sheet. Because the existence of such a situation might well affect a user's interpretation of the accounts it would seem reasonable for its existence if material to be suitably disclosed in the notes to the accounts.

The R.I.C.S. Guidance Notes continue:

> In the case of leasehold land and buildings, the total open market value will be the depreciable amount except where the future economic useful life of the buildings is less than the shorter of:
> (a) the unexpired term of the lease or an option to determine or extend the lease, or
> (b) the period remaining until a rent review to full annual value.
> Where the exception applies, the valuer would need to apportion his total value between the depreciable amount to be written off over the life of the buildings and the residual amount to be written off over the unexpired term of the lease or the period remaining until a rent review.

If there has been such an apportionment, and if the amount is material, it is suggested that the relevant facts should be disclosed in a note to the accounts.

Should valuations be incorporated in the accounts?

While it is probably generally agreed that it is useful to investors and other users of accounts to have up-to-date property values, there may be less agreement as to whether these should be incorporated in the accounts, or given in a note to the accounts on an analogy with the figure for market value of investments. Nor is it necessarily agreed that depreciation should be based on current values. Opponents of these ideas cite the fact that property values fluctuate (see Table 13 and Diagram 2) and that neither managers nor investors would want to take long term decisions on the best use of a company's property on the basis of short term fluctuations in value. (The short term for a decision relating to property in this instance would be about three to four years.)

Table 13					
Capital values (£ per sq. ft.) for owner-occupied vacant possession premises					
Year	Bristol	Southampton	Leeds	Manchester	Glasgow
1970	5.0	5.0	5.6	5.0	5.6
1971	6.5	—	6.5	—	—
1972	—	—	—	—	—
1973	10.0	11.4	9.3	8.6	—
1974	10.5	12.6	8.9	7.9	—
1975	13.0	13.5	10.3	10.3	13.0
1976	16.9	—	—	—	15.6
1977	18.6	17.2	17.2	18.6	18.6
1978	23.1	20.8	23.1	22.3	22.3
1979	29.2	38.3	27.5	27.5	26.7

— = not available

Source: Richard Ellis

Depreciation for costing and pricing purposes

It is very difficult to advise management on a suitable figure for depreciation for costing and pricing purposes. Prices should be based on an estimate of what the market will bear. For costing purposes it is desirable to use current values, and current estimates of residual life, but the following factors will militate against this:

(a) the fact that, usually, the buildings will not be replaced until many years have elapsed.

(b) depreciation on buildings is, usually, a very small part of total cost.

(c) competitive pressure on prices from other companies using historical cost figures to calculate depreciation.

(d) technological innovations mean that most buildings will be replaced by a completely different structure type.

35

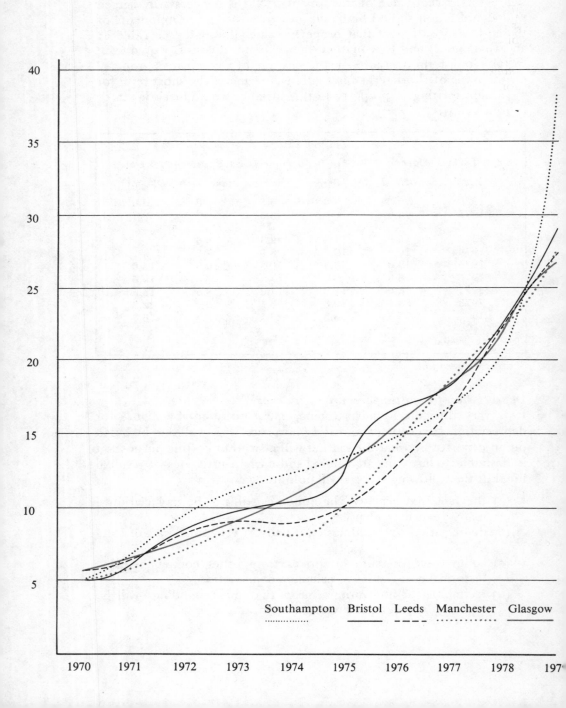

Diagram 2

Capital values (£s per sq. ft.) for owner occupied vacant
possession premises

Southampton   Bristol   Leeds   Manchester   Glasgow
....   − − − −   ....

1970   1971   1972   1973   1974   1975   1976   1977   1978   197

It is possible to use a notional rent for a similar property instead of depreciation. This would have the advantage that rents fluctuate less than property values. But rents include an element of interest on capital so there is a risk of double counting to be avoided.

Remaining life of property
In order to calculate the figure for depreciation it is not only necessary to consider what amount should be depreciated but also the length of time over which it should be depreciated. This sometimes gives rise to practical problems, three of which are discussed below.

Dominant and subservient structures
In a multi-structure complex buildings are often of different ages. Sooner or later some are going to require reconstruction.

A valuer can soon decide if a complex is capable of a rational division (and therefore separate reconstruction) or whether it is an integrated whole. Complexes capable of division should be considered as independent buildings (in groups) each group having a future economic useful life of its own.

Within those groups however there might be buildings of different ages and the concept of dominant or subservient structure should be developed. Take a five-year-old paint store in amongst a 50-year-old group of industrial buildings; this is subservient to the group and no doubt the directors took the view that they would have to write it off over a very short period when they authorised its construction. Obviously it will come down in, say, ten years when the rest of the adjoining group is redeveloped.

On the other hand, change the age of the paint store to 50 years and the industrial buildings to five years and there is a very different picture. In 10 years' time the paint store will have put into it a substantial capital injection to extend its life to co-terminate with the balance of the complex (the dominant structure).

Therefore the rule of thumb is that where the dominant structure has a shorter life expectancy than the subservient one, they should both be written off over the shorter (dominant life). Where the subservient structure has the shorter life expectancy, then the two structures should be independently written off over their individual lives (with it being anticipated that the subservient one will receive a future capital injection, which for the time being plays no part in the depreciation calculation, but which in future years, once done will be reflected).

Treatment of leaseholds

Leaseholds fall into many categories. In some instances the leases run beyond the life of the buildings, in which case the wasting element of value representing the buildings is written off over their future economic useful life, with the residual amount being written off over the entire lease. In other instances a lease is not as long as the future economic useful life of the building, in which case the value in its entirety is written off over the life of the lease alone.

Appreciation

In some unusual circumstances, where over-lettings are concerned or some other distortion has occurred, it may be possible that a lease has a strong negative value. In this case negative consumption occurs during the financial year. Negative consumption equals the appreciation during the year in question arising from the negative value having one year less to run than the year previously (this would apply to leaseholds to a greater extent than freeholds) although there are circumstances — such as onerous covenants — where a permanent negative value can be envisaged). The appreciation arising from the consumption of a negative value will be set off in the profit and loss account against depreciation in respect of other wasting assets.

III

The valuer's approach

6 The many values of a property

If users of accounts need to know the value of a company's property it is desirable to be precise as to which value, which user needs, and for what purpose. As a start, this Section sets out definitions of some of the more commonly used values.

(a) *Current open market value** is intended to mean the best price at which an interest in a property might reasonably be expected to be sold by Private Treaty at the date of valuation assuming:

- (i)   a willing seller
- (ii) a reasonable period within which to negotiate the sale, taking into account the nature of the property and the state of the market
- (iii) values will remain static throughout the period
- (iv) the property will be freely exposed to the market
- (v) no account is to be taken of an additional bid by a special purchaser †

(b) *Existing use value* is an open market value (see (a) above) but with the additional assumption that the property will continue in its existing use, and this ignores any possible alternative use of the

---

* Current OMV is sometimes referred to as OMV for sale.

† A special purchaser would perhaps be in the position to release latent potential, for instance by owning an adjoining property. The redevelopment of the merged sites could result in property with a greater value than the combined value of the two former properties. There are other possible special purchaser situations such as where the merging of tenures (e.g. freehold reversion plus lease in possession) throws up a value greater than the constituent parts.

property, any element of hope value*, any value attributable to goodwill and any possible increase in value due to special investment or financial transactions, such as sale and leaseback, which would leave the company with a different interest from the one which is to be valued.

Open market value for existing use would, however, include the possibilities of extensions or further buildings on undeveloped land or redevelopment of existing buildings, providing such construction can be undertaken without major interruption to the continuing business.

Existing use for the valuation of land and buildings in company accounts does not carry the same meaning as in planning law, or as current use for DLT purposes, nor does it necessarily mean the particular trade currently being undertaken on the property. Many buildings are general purpose structures suitable for a wide variety of different trades. Similar industrial buildings will probably have the same values irrespective of the different trades that are carried on, and this would also apply to shops. A factory is valued as a factory, not as a particular type of factory, and a shop as a shop, not as a particular type of shop (unless the market differentiates between the two).

If the property is a leasehold with a restrictive covenant, or is subject to a planning consent granted to the existing occupier only, then this would be ignored by the valuer who is concerned with the cost to the occupier to obtain a similar property.

However, the valuer should report to the directors the fact that the existence of the restrictive covenant etc. means that the alternative use value for the property is less than its existing use (see R.I.C.S. Background Paper on alternative use value). If the difference is material the directors should disclose it in their report or in a note to the accounts.

(c) *Alternative use value.* Some properties do not have any potential for any more valuable alternative use e.g. a city office block. Other properties could be used (after adaptation) for another use e.g. a warehouse for use as offices or a hospital for conversion to flats. The alternative use value is the value in the best alternative use, less the estimated costs of adaptation and conversion.

---

* Hope value is the result of an anticipation of an increase in value contingent on an event which may or may not happen e.g. obtaining planning permission or selling the property to someone who already owns an adjacent property.

(d) *Historical cost.* The price originally paid for the property, including acquisition costs and legal fees, plus any subsequent capital costs (i.e. improvements as opposed to maintenance — but see Section 10 below).

(e) *Depreciated replacement cost* is the gross replacement cost reduced to reflect the physical and functional obsolescence and environmental factors so as to arrive at the value of the building to the business at the relevant date plus the open market value of the land for existing use.

(f) *The gross replacement cost* is the estimated cost of erecting the building or a modern substitute building having the same gross internal area as that existing at prices current at the relevant date. This figure may include fees, finance charges appropriate to the construction period and other associated expenses directly related to the construction of the building.

(g) *Going concern value* is arrived at by capitalising the estimated maintained net earnings of the business. The R.I.C.S. have stated (Guidance Note A2(2) (iii)) that the expression 'going concern value' in relation to company property should not be used. However the R.I.C.S. admits that "there are some properties such as hotels, cinemas, theatres, bingo and gaming clubs, and petrol filling stations which are often sold only as a single entity to include the goodwill and fixtures and fittings" and for which it will therefore be difficult to obtain evidence of the value of the property separated from that of the business as a whole. A going concern value is the value of *all* the assets of the business and it would not be meaningful to endeavour to allocate it between the land and buildings and other assets. There is therefore a problem as to how much of the figure should be depreciated and at what rate.

It is always difficult to estimate the life of goodwill* and there are often tax considerations to be borne in mind in allocating a total purchase price.

* Accountants do not show internally generated goodwill in accounts because any valuation would be too subjective. Purchased goodwill (which may arise when one company buys another business for more than the 'value' of its tangible assets) is however shown in the accounts and may or may not be written off. One of the arguments used against writing off goodwill is that its value has been maintained by the purchasing company's activities. In my opinion this is fallacious because what has happened is that the original goodwill has decayed and been replaced by internally generated goodwill which accounting convention states should not be shown in the accounts.

41

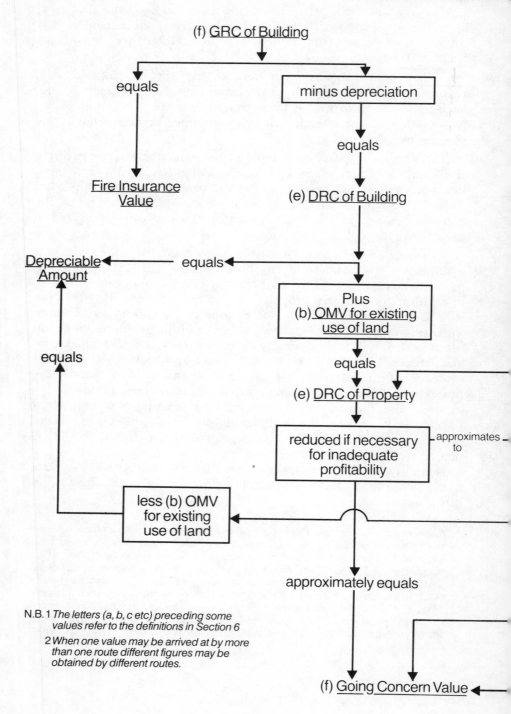

(f) <u>GRC of Building</u>

equals

minus depreciation

equals

Fire Insurance Value

(e) <u>DRC of Building</u>

<u>Depreciable Amount</u> ← equals ←

Plus
(b) <u>OMV for existing use of land</u>

equals

equals

(e) <u>DRC of Property</u>

reduced if necessary for inadequate profitability — approximates to

less (b) OMV for existing use of land

approximately equals

N.B. 1 *The letters (a, b, c etc) preceding some values refer to the definitions in Section 6*

2 *When one value may be arrived at by more than one route different figures may be obtained by different routes.*

(f) <u>Going Concern Value</u> ←

:TWEEN VALUES

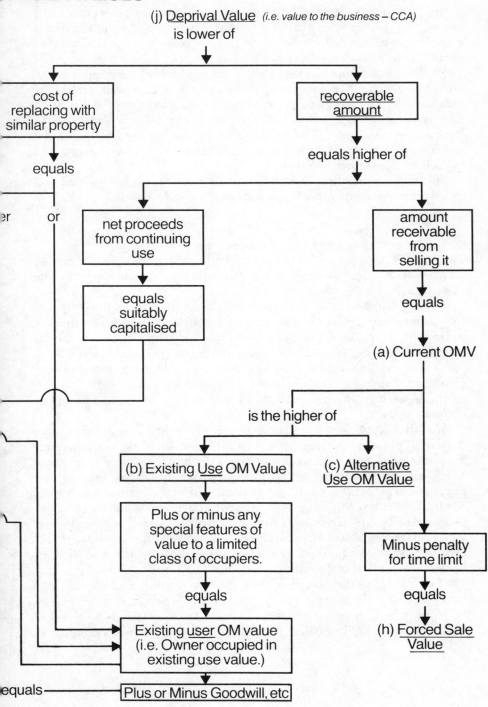

(j) <u>Deprival Value</u> *(i.e. value to the business – CCA)*
is lower of

cost of replacing with similar property

equals

<u>recoverable amount</u>

equals higher of

net proceeds from continuing use

equals suitably capitalised

amount receivable from selling it

equals

(a) Current OMV

is the higher of

(b) Existing <u>Use</u> OM Value

(c) <u>Alternative Use OM Value</u>

Plus or minus any special features of value to a limited class of occupiers.

equals

Minus penalty for time limit

equals

Existing <u>user</u> OM value (i.e. Owner occupied in existing use value.)

(h) <u>Forced Sale Value</u>

Plus or Minus Goodwill, etc

er   or

equals

(h) *Forced sale value* is the open market value (see (a) above) reduced by the proviso that the vendor has imposed a time limit for completion which cannot be regarded as a reasonable period as used in the definition of open market value.

(j) *Deprival value* is the loss that would be suffered by the company if it were deprived of the assets. This loss would be measured by the lower of (a) the cost of replacing the property with one of the same age, condition, and productive capacity, and (b) the 'recoverable amount'. The recoverable amount is the greater of the net proceeds from (i) continuing to use the asset in the business, and (ii) selling it to another business.

The relationship between these values and some others which will be introduced later in this book is illustrated in Diagram 3A.

Value in existing use or to the existing user

There would appear to be some uncertainty as to whether or not an 'existing use value' should reflect the value of the property to the existing *user*.

R.I.C.S. Guidance Note A2 uses the phrase 'the use of the property for the same purpose as hitherto' and goes on to say 'The market value under (a) above [existing use valuation] may include a special element attributable to the earning potential of the premises for a particular existing purpose by reason of their nature, location and character. Such element of value (if present) subsists irrespective of the benefit of the property to the particular undertaking of which it forms a part'.

But the R.I.C.S. background paper on existing use value says 'Existing use for the valuation of land and buildings in company accounts does not . . . necessarily mean the particular trade currently being undertaken on the property. Many buildings are general purpose structures suitable for a wide variety of different trades. Similar industrial buildings will probably have the same values irrespective of the different trades that are carried on, and this would also apply to shops. A factory is valued as a factory, not as a particular type of factory, and a shop as a shop, not as a particular type of shop (unless the market differentiates between the two)'.

The first quotation suggests that existing use value means existing user value, but the second quotation seems to be more restrictive.

The distinction between 'use' and 'user' is important as a use value may be more readily obtained in the market than a user value unless a similar user can be found. The distinction may be particularly important where the difference is the result of adaptation costs.

It would be desirable for the R.I.C.S. to clarify the distinction between

(a) open market value for existing *use*
(b) open market value to the existing *user*

Valuers sometimes use the phrase O.M.V. for existing use with vacant possession as if it were a synonym for O.M.V. for existing use. It may be equivalent to meaning (a) but not to meaning (b).

Accountants and users of accounts should be aware of the potential difference between (a) and (b) and make sure which of them is being provided by the valuer to the directors or by the directors in the accounts.

Balance sheet value
Given the fact that there are many values which can be legitimately applied to most properties, what is the meaning of 'balance sheet value'? It is the resultant of a mixture of the valuer's expertise and an accountant's conventions. Diagram 3B is a route map showing how a balance sheet value may be arrived at. Users of accounts will notice that there are at least seven possible different meanings to the phrase 'balance sheet value'. In addition the historical cost of a property is often referred as a balance sheet or book value! It will be seen that methods 2, 3, and 4 are based on valuations, method 6 on cost and valuation, and methods 1, 5, and 7 on estimated income. Balance sheet value is certainly a phrase to be used circumspectly.

Forced sale value, which appears on diagram 3A, is not shown on Diagram 3B although it might well be suitable for the balance sheet of a business which was not a 'going concern' i.e. one about which there were significant doubts concerning its viability. However a business in such a precarious position is not likely to be giving a high priority to preparing a balance sheet for publication.

7   Valuation methods

In arriving at one or more of the values of a property described in the previous Section, a valuer will use one or more of the following valuation methods:

(a) *Similar transactions* is the method preferred by the valuer. It is the evidence of recent sales or rent reviews of similar property.

A ROUTE MAP FOR ARRIVING AT A BALANCE SHEET VALUE*

DIAGRAM 3B

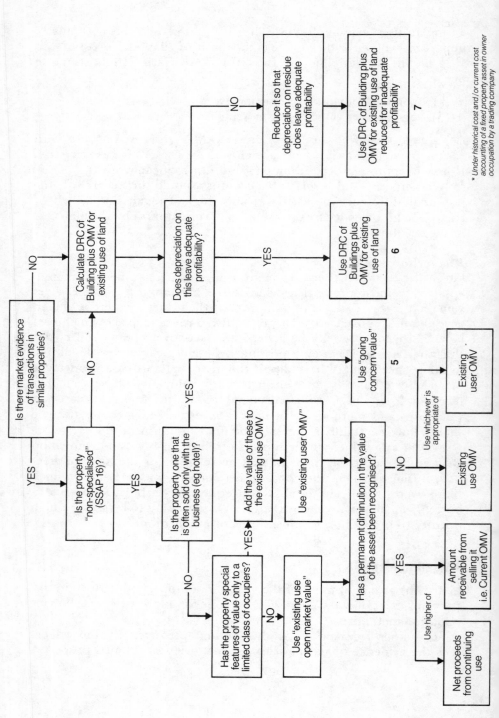

* Under historical cost and/or current cost accounting of a fixed property asset in owner occupation by a trading company

Such evidence will be obtained from sales or rent reviews negotiated by the valuer's own firm, contacts with other estate agents, press reports, discussions with other professionals in local government service or in taxation offices. It is a matter of skill and judgement as to what adjustments to make for differences between the property sold and the one being valued. The greater the length of time between the transaction and the date of valuation the less use it is as evidence. Whilst some evidence is of a capital nature, other is of a rental nature which then introduces the concept of converting this into a capital value (see (b) and (e) below).

(b) *Capitalised estimated rental value* is an investment multiplier applied to an entitlement to receive a notional or actual income. It is the yield on the property equity, e.g. a yield on a city office block may be 5% which equates to a multiplier of 20, that is 100 divided by 5. Twenty times the estimated rental value equals the capital value. The choice of a yield percentage is obviously a crucial matter of judgement and is based on evidence and experience of the property market.

The investment multiplier not only varies for different types of property investment (e.g. shops, offices etc.) but has also fluctuated over recent years with changes in demand and supply of property (see Table 14 and Diagrams 4 and 5). Demand for property comes

Table 14			
Schedule of Prime Investment Yields			
Year	*Offices* %	*Shops* %	*Industrials* %
1965	6½	6	9
1966	6½	6	9
1967	6½	6	9
1968	7	7	9
1969	6½	7	8¾
1970	7½	7½	9
1971	6¾	6¾	8½
1972	4	4	7½
1973	4¼	4½	7
1974	6½	6¾	9½
1975	6¾	7	9¼
1976	5¾	5¾	8
1977	5¼	5¼	7¼
1978	4¾	4¼	6½
1979	4¼	3¾	6

Source: Richard Ellis

47

not only from those who wish to occupy it but from those who wish to invest in it for income and/or capital appreciation. The demand for owner occupation is linked to the state of the economy in general and of particular sectors of it. The demand for investment property is also influenced by the weight of money seeking investment and the relative attraction of other investments.

(c) *Indexation of, and depreciation of, original cost* means applying a suitable index to the original cost of the property and then allowing for depreciation. The CSO publishes in 'Price Index Numbers for Current Cost Accounting':

(i) the old-established 'Index of the Cost of New Construction' which reflects mainly the costs of materials and labour, and is to be discontinued in due course; and

(ii) six 'Construction Output Price Indices' which are derived mainly from the prices of successful tenders (adjusted for the effect of 'Variation of Price' clauses and for the interval between tender and work done), and which more accurately reflect the cost to the customer of construction work currently done. There are separate indices for five broad types of new work and a composite index for all new construction work. These indices start in 1970, and the CSO recommends that they should be used in preference to the 'Index of the Cost of New Construction' from then onwards.

The index published by the Building Cost Information Service of the R.I.C.S. may also be used. This is based on actual tender prices.

The weaknesses of this method are that it assumes that the cost of constructing different properties rises to the same degree in all parts of the country, and that the value of land rises at the same rate as the cost of construction.

This method might be satisfactory for the interim updates between full revaluations envisaged by SSAP 16, and it could be applied to the wasting element in a D.R.C. valuation.

(d) *Depreciated replacement cost.* The cost of buying or constructing a property with the same operational capacity, but not necessarily by the same methods, is estimated. This is then reduced to allow for the age and condition of the property being valued. In addition to this reduction, other considerations can lead to further reductions in value, sometimes called 'end allowances', which would

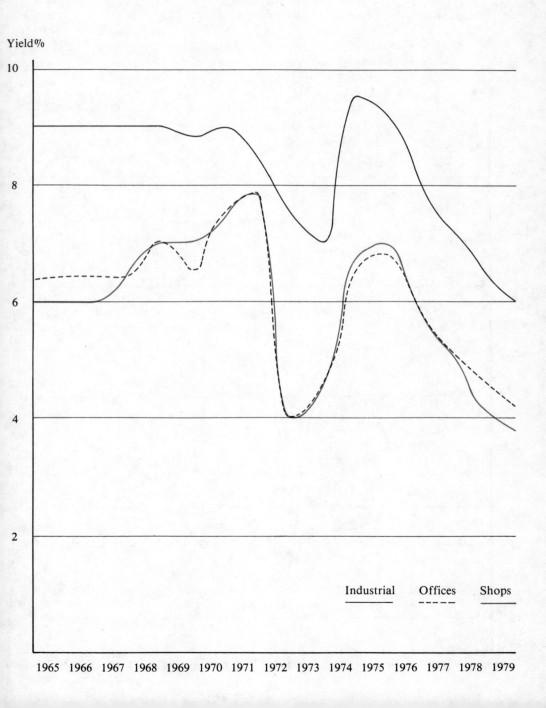

Diagram 4
Prime investment yields 1965–1979

Yield%

10

8

6

4

2

Industrial   Offices   Shops

1965 1966 1967 1968 1969 1970 1971 1972 1973 1974 1975 1976 1977 1978 1979

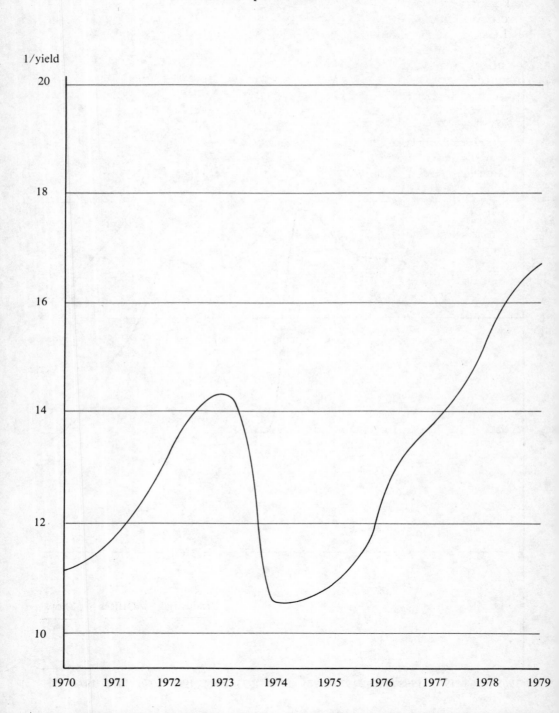

Diagram 5
Year's purchase since 1970

1/yield

20

18

16

14

12

10

1970 1971 1972 1973 1974 1975 1976 1977 1978 1979

take into account such factors as: obsolescence, size, site layout, overdevelopment, etc. Gross replacement cost is defined by the R.I.C.S. as the estimated cost of erecting the building or a modern substitute building having the same gross internal area as that existing at prices current at the relevant date. This figure may include fees, finance charges appropriate to the construction period and other associated expenses directly related to the construction of the building.

(e) *Discounted cash flow* is apparently not a method frequently used by property valuers as they consider that the forecast data is not sufficiently precise to warrant its use. It is a variant of the capitalised estimated rental method (see (b) above) but by using a suitable interest or discount rate allows for the fact that rents in future years are worth less now than rents for current years. This is because rents received now could be invested to earn interest during the period until future rents are received, whilst the future rents obviously could not be invested until they are received.

8 Valuation of property, land and buildings

At first sight it would seem that the value of the total property would be equal to the sum of the values of the land on which it is built and the buildings themselves. But it is not always, or indeed often, possible to arrive at the total value by summation.

In a depressed property market the value of the total property may well be pushed at least temporarily lower than the sum of the depreciated replacement cost of the buildings and the open market value of the bare site, because it would only be in exceptional circumstances that a bare site had a negative value. Although it must be remembered that the costs of demolition and clearing the site are unlikely to be negligible.

Similarly in a booming property market the value of the property may be pushed at least temporarily above the sum of the depreciated replacement cost of the buildings and the value of the land on which they are constructed, although the value of the land will tend to rise to restore the equality.

Time required for construction
One of the main reasons for this economic phenomenon is the long time taken to construct a new commercial building. The time from purchase of site to the occupier being able to use the building is

usually measured in years. A typical range would be 1 to 3 years. This means that the supply of *new* property is inevitably sluggish in its response to changes in demand for property, with the consequence that the price of *existing* property is more volatile than the price of its two constituents — land and new buildings. In the long run the sale value of property for which there is a significant demand must be linked to the costs of construction of buildings and purchase of land. In the short term there may well be divergences which lead to the volatile nature of property developers' profits.

Developers' risk
Another reason for the value of the property not being equal to the sum of the values of land and buildings is the profit expected by the developer. This profit relates partly to the exposure risk incurred by the developer, and he will take into account, in assessing the profit he requires, the time period over which his exposure will last, the gross amount of capital at risk, the margin between the likely costs and the likely end value, and the quality of the investment. There is no rule of thumb to determine developer's profit which will depend partly on competition among developers. The risk involved in development is a factor which must be taken into account in the relationship between the value of the land and the cost of the buildings on the one hand and the open market valuation of the property on the other.

The foregoing may be summed up in the following formulae:

(1) $P_c = B_b + L_a + DP_b$

(2) $L_e = P_a - DC_d$

where
P = Value of property
B = Cost of building
L = Value of land
DP = Developer's profit
DC = Demolition costs
a = now
b = time taken to construct
c = end of period b
d = time taken to demolish
e = end of period d

Leaseholds

Leaseholds can have a negative value when the rent payable under them is higher than the present market rent or when the cost of reinstating the property at the end of the lease is likely to be high in relation to the rent payable and the market rent.

Problems of arriving at a basis for depreciation

This lack of equality between the value of the property, and the value of the land and buildings of which it is composed, can cause problems in discussions between valuers, accountants and business-men when a figure for the value of buildings is required for the purposes of calculating depreciation in accordance with SSAP 12. The R.I.C.S. in its Guidance Note J1 is careful to avoid the impression that an open market value of a property can be divided into one figure for buildings and one for land with no remainder (positive or negative), as the following quotation shows. "When providing figures for the purposes of depreciation, the valuer should emphasise in the report, that the resultant figures, i.e. the depreciable amount and the residual amount are informal apportionments and that the individual figures do not represent the open market value of the building and land elements".

This subject has, however, already been discussed in Section 5 above and is also discussed in a recent article by C. Noke (The reality of property depreciation, *Accountancy*, November 1979).

An economist's view

Turvey* believes that any attempt to divide 'property' into 'land' and 'buildings' has no analytical value, and is meaningless except in long-run stationary equilibrium. He argues as follows:

The following magnitudes can be ascertained or estimated:
T = the market value of a building on a site,
R = the replacement cost of the building,
T' = the market value the property would have if the building on it were new and represented the highest and best (most profitable) use of the site,
C = the cost of constructing such a building,
S = T'−C, market value of the site.

If S exceeds T by more than the cost of demolition (net of scrap value), it will pay to demolish the building. Thus it might be said that T could be divided into S and (T−S) the value of the building, since if (T−S) is positive it represents

* *The Economics of Real Property*, Allen & Unwin, 1957, p. 23.

53

the sum which would just compensate the owner for removal of the building. Nobody, however, will ever offer to pay (T—S)†, so it is not in any sense a 'market' value.

Alternatively, it might be said that T could be divided between R, the value of the building, and (T—R), the value of the site. But R may be irrelevant to any proposed action, so cannot be called a 'market' value. Thus neither method of division has any useful meaning except in the event of their coincidence, when:

$$S = T—R$$

which requires that:

$$T'—C = T—R$$

Apart from coincidence, the only general case where this equality is fulfilled seems to be where the existing building is that representing the highest and best use (so that $T = T'$) and is new (so that $C = R$). But then the division is useless since one can simply speak of S, site value, C, construction cost, and T, market value of the property. T will equal S + C in a competitive market, if a developer's profit is included in C.

The two divisions will thus be consistent only in the long-run stationary equilibrium. But since building value is defined residually and since its equality with R only follows from the assumption that there is equilibrium, the concept is useless for economic analysis. Since no ordinary building is ever sold floating in the air, this is not surprising.

9 Comparability of valuations

We have already seen (in Section 6) that a single property can have many different valuations. But how many of these valuations give the same figure? To what extent is it possible for a business to save on valuers' fees by using a valuation prepared for one purpose (e.g. fire insurance) for another purpose (e.g. balance sheet valuation)?

It will be remembered (page 12 above) that the R.I.C.S. Guidance Note A2 says that all property valuations for disclosure in directors' reports or accounts should be 'open market valuations' except in the case of some kinds of property (e.g. chemical works) which are rarely (if ever) sold except by way of sale of the business as a whole. In such cases the valuation should be made by the depreciated replacement cost (D.R.C.) method (page 48 above).

There appears however to be a growing movement in some valuation circles to extend the use of D.R.C. valuations using the argument that it is not only quarries with lime kilns which are rarely if ever sold, but also large and unwieldy premises such as awkwardly planned factories or unusual developments such as television studios. Carrying the D.R.C. argument to its fullest extent, a case could be made out perhaps for every property to have a uniqueness which

† Because of the impossibility of physically separating land from buildings.

prevents it from being valued by reference to comparable evidence on the open market and that in the future it may be that D.R.C. becomes the only recognised method of balance sheet valuation.

However, before this comes to pass it must be noted that D.R.C. often produces figures very different from open market value. For instance, in a border-line case concerning a very substantial food preparation factory of approximately 600,000 sq. ft., arguments might be put forward for valuing either by reference to open market transactions or by reference to depreciated replacement cost.

Assuming the open market method were to be used, it is generally agreed by valuers that there would be a substantial discount for quantum* as would be evidenced by other transactions of similarly large properties. In this instance a capital valuation of £4.5m might result. Applying the D.R.C. method to the same premises (even assuming a fairly short remaining economic useful life) a figure of over £6.5m might result (for details see next page).

The conceptual question which worries the valuers, concerns which figure should be entered into the balance sheet (£4.5m or £6.5m). The accounts in fact incorporated the higher figure — no doubt influenced by the historic expenditure used to create the complex. If the premises were to have been offered for sale on the open market it is doubtful whether a purchaser could have been obtained on the basis of a continuation of the existing use. It is probable that some demolition and rationalisation would take place and the highest figure obtainable on the open market might be only £3.5m. (A forced sale might discount this figure to £3.0m.)

The following example is also drawn from a valuation by Richard Ellis.

The property concerned is a private hospital being part of a group of hospitals. The group as a whole aims to break even and therefore does not maximise potential profit. The property in the example makes a small profit on an annual basis. It was built from locally raised subscriptions. The balance sheet value is on the basis of existing use reduced for low profitability (£40,000). However if profits were maximised a purchaser might be prepared to pay considerably more for it still in the existing use (£140,000) as a hospital or, if there was no way of increasing income and/or reducing outgoings, it might be bought on the basis of alternative use (£115,000). It will

* A discount for quantum reflects the fact that a very large building is less easy to sell and will therefore have a lower value per square foot. Large in this instance would be a building with an area in excess of about 500,000 sq. ft.

Example

The property comprises food processing factory of 600,000 sq. ft. on approximately 21 acre site. Site is overdeveloped and restricted in access and manoeuvrability.

Buildings on site vary from 1890's stone office block, to three storey production/storage buildings, to 1960's single span packing and storage units.

Situated in an industrial/warehouse area with good access to main distributor roads. In an area of current high demand.

Comments

1. Open market comparable rents range between 75p and £1.75p per sq. ft. There is a discount for very large structures and 15% is assumed to be appropriate. Current yields for comparable properties are about 13.3%.

2. For the depreciated replacement cost calculation, it is assumed that the company could reduce the floor space of the three storey block by one third by utilising a modern equivalent.* Although the whole site might take four years to develop, it is assumed that some buildings could be brought into production before that date, therefore finance has been taken over two years on half building cost and fees. A future economic useful life of 20 years for all buildings is adopted as redevelopment as a whole would take place rather than piecemeal redevelopment. The land is valued on the basis of comparable cleared site evidence.

Valuation No. 1 by comparable method

Ref.	Sq. Ft.	Rent per Sq. Ft.	Rent per Annum
3 storey Production Building	254,322	£0.75p	£ 190,741
Single storey 1940's Production Building	103,799	£1.10p	£ 114,179
Single storey 1960's	181,098	£1.70p	£ 307,867
Offices	20,126	£1.75p	£ 35,220
Admin.	26,535	£1.75p	£ 46,436
Ancillary	12,690	£0.70p	£ 8,883
	598,570		£ 703,326
Discount of 15%			£ 105,499
			£ 597,827
y.p. (13.33%)			7.5
			£4,483,702
			TOTAL SAY £4.5m

Valuation No. 2 by D.R.C. method

Ref.	Building Cost per Sq. Ft.	Gross Building Cost	Fees 12½%	Interest 12% 2 yrs on ½ cost	Total	Notional Age of Buildings	Future Economic Useful Life	Factor	D.R.C.
3 storey Production Building	£12	£2,034,576*	£254,322	£291,148	£2,580,046	40	20	20/60	£ 860,015
Single storey 1940's Production Building	£12	£1,245,588	£155,698	£178,244	£1,579,530	40	20	20/60	£ 526,510
Single storey 1960's	£12	£2,173,176	£271,647	£310,981	£2,755,804	15	20	20/35	£1,574,745
Offices	£25	£ 503,150	£ 62,894	£ 72,001	£ 638,045	40	20	20/60	£ 212,682
Admin.	£20	£ 530,700	£ 66,338	£ 75,943	£ 672,981	35	20	20/55	£ 244,720
Ancillary	£12	£ 152,280	£ 19,035	£ 21,791	£ 193,106	40	20	20/60	£ 64,369
		£6,639,470			£8,419,512				£3,483,041

Land Valuation
19 acres (main)	@ £150,000	£2,850,000
2 acres (ancillary)	@ £100,000	£ 200,000
		£3,050,000
		£6,533,041
	TOTAL	SAY £6.5m

56

be noted that the property would cost considerably more than any disposal price to rebuild currently (£1,250,000).

The O.M.V. in existing use is less than the O.M.V. for sale because of the low profitability of the existing use. The question of reducing valuations for inadequate profitability is discussed on page 67 below.

Summary	Value	% of lowest property figure
Open market value for sale	£ 140,000	350
Open market value in existing use	£ 140,000	350
Open market value to existing user (reduced for low profitability)	£ 40,000	100
Open market value alternative use	£ 115,000	288
Gross replacement cost (Building GRC £1,250,000 + Land OMV £100,000)	£1,350,000	3,375
Depreciated replacement cost (Building DRC £700,000 + Land OMV £100,000)	£ 800,000	2,000
Fire insurance value (excluding consequential loss)	£1,250,000	3,125
Forced sale value	£ 120,000	300
Going concern value	£ 40,000	100
Deprival value — OM route	£ 40,000	100
— DRC route	£ 800,000	2,000
— DRC route reduced for inadequate profitability	£ 40,000	100
Depreciable amount (OMV minus land)	—	—
Depreciable amount (DRC of buildings)	£ 700,000	1,750

The food processing factory quoted above was found to have the following values:

	Value	% of lowest property figure
Open market value for sale	£ 3.5m	117
Open market value in existing use	£ 3.5m	117
Open market value to existing user	£ 4.5m	150
Open market value in alternative use	£ 3.5m	117
Gross replacement cost (Building GRC £8.4m + Land OMV £3.05m)	£11.45m	382
Depreciated replacement cost (Building DRC £3.48m + Land OMV £3.05m)	£ 6.5m	217
Fire insurance value (excluding consequential loss)	£ 8.4m	280

57

	Value	% of lowest property figure
Forced sale value	£ 3.0m	100
Going concern value	£ 6.5m	217
Deprival value — OM route	£ 4.5m	150
— DRC route	£ 6.5m	217
Depreciable amount (OMV minus land)	£ 1.45m	48
Depreciable amount (DRC of buildings)	£ 3.48m	116

The above examples illustrate the dangers of using values prepared for one purpose for another purpose, and the importance of the user knowing the basis of any valuation. It should, however, be pointed out that, provided the valuer is asked to provide valuations on a number of different bases at the beginning of his assignment, the number of bases would not normally add significantly to the fee.

IV

The interface between valuers and accountants

10 Some problems shared by valuers and accountants

The problem of separating property from plant
When valuing a property it is usual for a valuer to include in his valuation certain items of plant. There is a possibility that some of these items of plant may have been included by the company's accountant in the company's balance sheet figure for plant and machinery. There is thus a risk that the same plant may appear twice in the balance sheet and overstate the 'value' of a company's assets and its figure for depreciation.

Guidance is given to valuers on this subject by the R.I.C.S. in Note F2 (reproduced in appendix 5). The types of plant most likely to be involved are: items for the transmission or storage of electricity, gas, and water; heating and ventilating plant; lifts and gantries.

It is important that there should be adequate liaison between valuer, accountant and auditor to avoid double counting.

The problem of repairs
A related problem occurs when certain items of expenditure on the property (e.g. repairs) have been written off, quite properly, in the profit and loss account for tax or other reasons, but which have in fact increased the value of the property as shown by a subsequent valuation either because they have extended its economic life or because they contain an element of improvement even though treated as being all repairs. If the valuation is then used as a basis for depreciation it would appear that the item is being charged to profit and loss account twice; once as a cost and once as depreciation. The company would also show an increase in property values which

would owe more to accounting methods than to any 'real' changes in value and might therefore be misleading.

The problem therefore is in the allocation of the reserves between those that are realised (distributable) and those that are unrealised (undistributable). The writing off of the 'repairs' underrates the distributable reserves, although the transfers between the reserves arising from the depreciation charged on the revalued amount will correct the allocation over the remaining useful life of the property.

Conversely, a company may neglect to carry out repairs and thus increase reported profit whilst the deterioration in the 'value' of the property is not revealed either because the property is not revalued or because the drop in 'real' value is masked by the effects of inflation. This could lead to over-distribution of realised profits.

The problem of interim valuations

SSAP 16 may create further problems at the interface between valuers, accountants and auditors when it suggests (Guidance Notes on SSAP 16: Current Cost Accounting, paragraph 40) that it will be possible for directors and/or valuers to provide updated valuations between the major revaluations at approximately five yearly intervals.*

This suggestion may create the impression that a valuer may be able to provide, for a small fee, an overall percentage to apply to the previous valuation. Whilst indexation of the building element in a D.R.C. valuation may give a reasonably meaningful answer, it is unlikely that indexation of an open market valuation would. It is unrealistic to expect property prices to move uniformly — there are differences between types of property and between locations. Valuers can however provide annual updates for much less than the initial valuation fee (see page   below).

Valuers can also provide directors with a letter saying that there has been no material change in the value of the property since it was last valued. However, a valuer will only be prepared to sign such a letter if the originating valuation was carried out by the valuer's firm and when there have been no material changes not only in the market, but also relating to tenure, the physical state of the property, planning matters, the law, etc.

---

* See "Procedures for reviewing previous valuations", *Chartered Surveyor*, November 1979, p.120.

Government grants
SSAP 4 says:

Grants relating to fixed assets should be credited to revenue over the expected useful life of the asset. This may be achieved by:

    (a) reducing the cost of the acquisition of the fixed asset by the amount of the grant; or

    (b) treating the amount of the grant as a deferred credit, a portion of which is transferred to revenue annually.

If method (b) is selected, the amount of the deferred credit should, if material, be shown separately in the balance sheet. It should not be shown as part of shareholders' funds.

The *Survey of Published Accounts 1978* shows that, of the 300 large companies surveyed which disclosed their policy for accounting for grants approximately half (181 companies) used method (a) and half used method (b).

The valuer, however, makes no deduction from a depreciated replacement cost valuation for any capital based government grant potentially receivable at the date of valuation. The existence of such grants in a particular area may however depress second-hand property prices.

This combination of approaches could therefore lead to a 'surplus on revaluation' which again could have resulted more from accounting and valuation methods than from any changes in 'real values'. Directors, accountants, and auditors may need to consider the implications of such a situation for the 'true and fair view' when reporting the surplus on revaluation.

It must be remembered that Regional Development Grants are repayable, in whole or in part, in some circumstances. E.g.

    (a) Asset not brought into use within six months.

    (b) Asset destroyed or ceased to be used within one year.

    (c) The premises concerned cease to be used for qualifying activities within four years (five years for agricultural property).

Full details should be obtained from the Department of Industry.

V

The user's needs and problems

11 What is a balance sheet valuation?

Let us start to answer the above question by trying to define an asset. A working definition might be "an economic sacrifice for which an expected potential benefit has not yet been realised". At the date of acquisition the value of the sacrifice is probably the historical cost, at the time of disposal or retirement the value of the asset is again quantified at what it was sold for. The problem is what to do in between these two events. One answer is that perhaps the value during this period — "the economic sacrifice for which a potential benefit has not yet been realised" — is the opportunity foregone by continued ownership and use for the business as opposed to selling the property to someone else. This would mean that the value would be the *sale price* less selling expenses. But a balance sheet valuation is usually based on O.M.V. for *existing use* which may be lower than the O.M.V. for sale (see pages 39 et seq above).

Another way of looking at the problem is to say that a property has basically only three values relevant to answering the question posed in the title to this Section. They are:

$$V_S = \text{Sale value}$$

$$V_B = \text{Cost to buy or build a similar property}$$

$$V_U = \text{Value to present owner in use}$$

V_S will equal the greater of the R.I.C.S. definition of open market value for existing use and the open market value in alternative use.

V_B will equal the cost of buying and existing similar property, or in the absence of comparable evidence, may be estimated as the sum of the depreciated replacement cost of the buildings and the open market value of the site for its existing use.

V_U is the value of the property in its current use. It will equal the minimum sum which a reasonable director would be willing to accept in compensation for compulsory acquisition of the property alone as a business asset i.e. ignoring any higher value in an alternative use.* V_U could be measured in theory by calculating the going concern value of the whole business and subtracting from that the value of all items which can be removed from the premises, including goodwill unless it attaches to the premises rather than the business.

Because of transaction costs, it is reasonable to assume that V_S is less than V_B, but V_S in an alternative use may be higher than V_B in the existing use.

Given the above (and they are all obviously debatable) there are three main possible situations (ignoring equalities):

1. $V_U < V_S$ (where $<$ means 'less than')

2. $V_S < V_U < V_B$

3. $V_B < V_U$

In the first situation a wholly rational director would advocate selling the property, but it would be important to consider the disruption costs of selling one property and buying and moving to another. What would the effects of such a move be on (a) the existing work force — how many of them would move with the company, (b) the company's operating costs, and (c) its relationships with customers and suppliers?

In this situation it could be argued that the revaluation of the property to be incorporated in the balance sheet should be V_S, or, more precisely, V_S minus disruption costs. It will be recognised that this is the situation where a company is potentially vulnerable to a takeover bid or to an asset stripping operation.

An auditor might well have difficulty in verifying the size of the estimated disruption costs as fear of an unwelcome bid could lead to their size being exaggerated.

The second situation would suggest that the company would continue to use the property, but would not replace it if deprived of it now, or at the end of its economic life if relative values had not changed. In this situation the revaluation in the balance sheet would be V_U.

---

* Legislation dealing with compulsory purchase provides for additional sums to be paid for removal expenses, interest, goodwill, stock, etc.

In the third situation a company would continue to use the property, and replace it if deprived of it now, or at the end of its life if relative values had not changed. In this situation the valuation in its balance sheet would be $V_{\bar{B}}$.

But how far apart, in practice, are V_S and V_B? In the U.K. the difference is generally small — about 5% — but in countries such as France the difference may be as great as 20%. The difference between V_S and V_B is greater for special purpose buildings which are not readily marketable. V_S may also deviate markedly from V_B where V_B has been derived from a D.R.C. calculation.

V_U may be materially higher than V_S when planning permission has been granted only to the present user.

12 Value of the property, or value of the property to the business

The accountant is aware that a balance sheet under the historical cost convention is not a statement of the values of the assets and liabilities of the business. Even if it were, the value of the business could easily be greater or less than the net sum of the values of its assets and liabilities. It is important, however, to consider what the user of published accounts believes a balance sheet to be and what he would like it to be.

Shareholders' understanding of accounts
Lee and Tweedie found* that the understanding of shareholders of a balance sheet was as follows:

Reasonable	37%
Vague	21%
None	42%

However the shareholders' statements were concerned with the items included in the balance sheet and not with their valuation, as the following extract‡ from Lee and Tweedie's study shows.

* op. cit, p.36.
‡ Ibid p.160.

Contents of balance sheet stated to include:

assets only	9%
liabilities and/or share capital only	3%
details of liquidity or working capital	3%
assets and liabilities	27%
assets, liabilities, and net worth	11%
financial state of company at a point in time	4%
Other answers	2%
Obviously incorrect answers	19%
'Do not knows' and 'no answers'	23%
	101%*

*   4 respondents (1% of 301) gave two content items.

All of the above mentioned specific items were classified as correct answers, and certain of the 'other answers' were also classified as correct. *Reasonable understanding* was attributed to those respondents who either gave the fourth or fifth-mentioned specific item, provided no incorrect item was also given. *Vague understanding* was attributable to those respondents who gave either one of the other specific items (with no incorrect answer given) or who gave two correct and one incorrect items. The remaining respondents were classified as having *no understanding*.

Lee and Tweedie did not ask a question about property valuation but did ask about plant valuation with the following results.*

	%	%
Reasonable understanding		
Original cost less depreciation		70
Vague understanding		
Original cost		3
No understanding		
Replacement cost	7	
Realizable value	3	
Original cost and replacement cost or realizable value	1	
Other incorrect answers	1	
'Do not knows' and 'no answers'	15	27
		100

In reply to a question on the main purposes of financial statements the following answers were given.†

*   Ibid, p.166.
†   Ibid, p.155.

	%	%
Reasonable understanding		
Accountability to shareholders	27	
Data for investment decisions	<u>15</u>	42‡
Vague understanding		
Justification for dividends	3	
Vague answers indicating accountability	<u>4</u>	7
No understanding		
Data for Inland Revenue	3	
Indicate value of company	30	
Indicate market value of shares	6	
Fulfilling a legal obligation	12	
Keeping people informed	19	
Other answers (including 'do not know' and 'no answers')	<u>14</u>	<u>84</u>
		133§

‡ 46 of these respondents (15% of 301) gave a reasonable answer coupled with an incorrect one, and were re-designated for other purposes as having a vague understanding.

§ 76 respondents (25% of 301) indicated two objectives, and 12 respondents (4% of 301) indicated three objectives.

It should be noted that 36% believed that the accounts indicated the *value* of the company or its shares.

In the light of the above it is perhaps not surprising that one of Lee and Tweedie's recommendations is to "provide the private shareholder with a reasonable understanding of the balance sheet in particular".

"Private shareholders should be more aware of the articulation of the balance sheet and profit and loss account and, particularly, the present use by the reporting accountant of the balance sheet as a statement of balances appearing in the accounting records".* It would certainly seem that directors, valuers and auditors should make an especial effort to explain to shareholders the basis of valuation of property.

Value in existing or alternative use
Let us now return to what is shown in the accounts as opposed to what shareholders believe is shown by them.

The value of the property to a business in its present use (V_U) may be materially less than the value in an alternative use or the

* Ibid, p.133.

66

depreciated replacement cost. In this situation the accounting convention would be to show V_U in the balance sheet. The wording of the relevant part of SSAP 12 is as follows: "... if at any time the unamortised cost of an asset is seen to be irrecoverable in full, it should be written down immediately to the estimated recoverable amount..." (SSAP 12 para 18).

Such a write down would be shown as part of the charge for depreciation. If material it should be disclosed as an exceptional item.

Adequate profitability

The R.I.C.S. Guidance Note A2 states that if the existing use value has had to be estimated by using the depreciated replacement cost method then "such valuation should be expressed as subject to adequate profitability related to the value of the total assets" A2(2)(iv). Curiously, this caveat does not appear to be suggested for an 'open market valuation', although it is not unimaginable that such a method could also show an inadequate return on capital.

An O.M.V. is based on market information, whilst a D.R.C. valuation is more hypothetical so the need for such a caveat may be greater for a D.R.C. valuation, but the difference in treatment could well be significant to the user of the accounts. It will be remembered that the O.M.V. for existing *use* does not relate to the existing *user's* profitability. An O.M.V. for existing use may well exceed the O.M.V. for alternative use for the same property (see e.g. page 57).

There is a significant difference in the wording of SSAP 12 and A2. SSAP 12 used the phrase "irrecoverable in full" which would presumably only be invoked if profitability were to fall below zero. A2 refers to "adequate profitability" which would presumably apply above a zero rate of return.* Adequate profitability is not defined but would presumably be related to (a) the current rate of money return on a relatively risk free investment (e.g. a bank deposit account), (b) the rate of inflation, (c) the degree of risk of the business concerned.

So there are possible practical situations where the value of the property in the balance sheet (V_U) is less than the value of the property measured by V_S or V_B. What is worrying is that it appears

* The Guidance Notes on Valuation of the Incorporated Society of Valuers and Auctioneers makes no reference to a reduction for inadequate profitability in its definition of Depreciated Replacement Cost.

that the user of accounts is unlikely to be informed of the existence of this situation, its magnitude or implications despite the existence of s16 of the 1967 Companies Act. This could lead to an unwittingly circular argument by a user of published accounts. Let us assume that a valuer uses the depreciated replacement cost method of valuation for a company's property; this value is then, quite properly, reduced because of the 'adequate profitability' test, but the fact of the reduction is not mentioned in the accounts. An analyst then calculates the company's return on capital and will inevitably find it as adequate as the directors' own calculation. On the strength of this he may recommend a purchase of the share but the company is in fact heading for potential trouble in that it is not earning enough to finance the replacement of its property out of profits.

It would seem highly desirable therefore that directors should be obliged to disclose in the notes to the accounts:

(a) how much of a property valuation is on a depreciated replacement cost basis, and

(b) how much this has been reduced because of the application of the adequate profitability test, and

(c) if (b) applies how 'adequate profitability' is defined.

A possible snag for implementing such a proposal would be that directors could avoid making the recommended disclosure by describing the reduced valuation as their own and not as the valuers' and not giving the basis of their valuation.

Another alternative would be to prohibit reductions of valuations outside the accounts and to require such a reduction to be made as an exceptional item in the profit and loss account.

13 Materiality

Two questions need to be posed on behalf of the users of published accounts:

(a) How material is property in the balance sheet of a non-property company, and how material is the depreciation on it in relation to profit?

(b) How large are valuers' fees in relation to the benefit of having a current value of property?

Materiality of property and depreciation

In order to get an answer to question (a) we took a random sample of 43 recent accounts of Dearden Farrow's clients (large and small) which are not property companies and calculated the median, upper and lower quartiles or highest and lowest, for the following ratios for the 30 companies which had not had a recent revaluation and for the 13 which had.

1. Value of property/value of all fixed and current assets (%).
2. Depreciation of property/profit before tax and extraordinary items (%).
3. Depreciation of property/profit after tax and extraordinary items (%).
4. Depreciation of property/turnover (%).
5. Depreciation of property/per employee (£ per head).
6. Depreciation of property/wages and salaries (%).

The figures in Table 15 indicate that, as would be expected there is a fairly wide range for all the ratios, with those for companies with a recent valuation being higher than those without.

There would appear to be little doubt of the materiality of property in the balance sheet (ratio 1).

The materiality of depreciation (ratios 2 to 6) is less certain for most companies. This evidence is particularly relevant to the recommendation that is made on page 83 that depreciation should be calculated on the whole value of the property and not on an artificial split between 'land' and 'buildings'.

Materiality of valuers' fees

There is no hard and fast rule on fees from a valuer's point of view. It depends very much on circumstances and on the nature of the portfolio. Some portfolios could comprise for instance 100 provincial secondary shops whilst other portfolios could have three London factories. The recommended R.I.C.S. fee is value based and reads as follows (partial quote):

'A) *Freehold property*
1%   on the first £1,500
0.5%   on the next £11,000
0.25% on the residue of the valuation of the freehold'.

This fee base is in many cases unworkable and Richard Ellis normally relate their professional charges to time sheets kept on jobs.

Table 15

Materiality of property and depreciation

Ratio	Recent Valuation			No Recent Valuation		
	Lower Quartile	Median	Upper Quartile	Lower Quartile	Median	Upper Quartile
1) Value of property/ value of all fixed and current assets (%).	12.73	24.61	31.63	9.54	13.82	30.18
2) Depreciation of property/profit before tax and extraordinary items (%).	2.05	3.16	4.98	1.26	3.07	5.54
3) Depreciation of property/profit after tax and extraordinary items (%).	2.56	3.80	8.01	1.96	5.85	10.43
4) Depreciation of property/turn-over (%).	0.07	0.23	0.57	0.118	0.177	0.41
5) Depreciation of property/per employee (£ per head).	36.39*	79.33	132.65*	15.35	26.57	53.09
6) Depreciation of property/wages and salaries (%).	0.87	1.51	4.46	0.465	0.92	1.83

* = lowest and highest in the range

To assess the materiality of valuers' fees a random sample was taken of 31 valuations conducted by Richard Ellis in the last few years and the following ratios were calculated:

1. Fee/value (%).
2. Fee/turnover (%).
3. Fee/profit before tax (%).
4. Fee/employee (£/head).
5. Fee/wages and salaries (%).

70

The results are shown in Table 16 separately for valuations and revaluations.

Table 16							
Materiality of valuers' fees							
	Valuations				Revaluations		
	Lower Quartile	Median	Upper Quartile	No. of valuations	Lower Quartile	Median	Upper Quartile	No. of revaluations
Fee/value %	0.135	0.252	0.306	31	0.0203	0.0609	0.164	20
Fee/turnover %	0.0162	0.0508	0.411	16	0.0311	0.198	0.495	16
Fee/profit before tax %	0.331	1.19	2.41	18	0.0488	4.28	15.8	19
Fee/no. of employees £/head.	5.09	8.47	27.0	15	0.196	4.57	8.94	10
Fee/wages & salaries %	0.148	0.457	1.775	14	0.0806	0.115	0.297	7

The ratio of the revaluation fee to the original valuation fee was also calculated with the following result:

Lower quartile	25.2%
Median	41.8%
Upper quartile	52.6%

The figures in Table 16 should be used with a certain amount of caution for two reasons:

(a) The figure for the fee used for all calculations included in some cases a charge for work in addition to a balance sheet valuation (e.g. a rental schedule for inter-company leases, depreciation for SSAP 12, depreciation for Hyde, Fire Insurance Valuations).

71

(b) Some of the portfolios contain leaseholds. Properties which are leasehold are charged on a valuation scale, which not only takes into account the capital value of the lease but also of the rent passing. Let us take for example a very substantial office property with a current rental value of £1m. per annum, which has been let to a tenant on long lease at half a million pounds per annum. The valuer would capitalise the profit rent* for the unexpired term, but would charge a fee not only relating to the capital value reported but also relating to the rent passing. The reason behind this is that the valuer has had to value a building with a rental value of £1m. per annum. If freehold, such a building would be worth upwards of £15m. (£1m. per annum at 15 years' purchase), although the figure reported to the leasehold occupier may only be £4m. or £5m. as being the suitably capitalised value of his profit rent.

Readers will no doubt form their own views on materiality of these fees but they certainly seem to support the view that the valuers' fee is not likely to be substantial in relation to the value of the property or the size of the business. Moreover, revaluations are much less expensive than valuations — most fall between a quarter and a half of the original fee.

14 Cost and benefits of a valuation

The benefit from using a Chartered Surveyor to produce an up-to-date value for a company property is not limited to being able to put a realistic figure in the balance sheet. The costs of a valuation are described in Section 13 on Materiality (page 69 above). The benefits include obtaining information on:

(a) alternative and more profitable uses for the property
(b) need for maintenance
(c) possible under-insurance against loss from fire
(d) possible reductions in rateable value
(e) realistic values for management accounts for pricing and location decisions
(f) scope for increased borrowing
(g) vulnerability to takeover bids and asset strippers

* The difference between the rent the tenant pays and the current open market rent. In this example the figures are £½m. and £1m. respectively giving a profit rent of £½m.

72

(h) existence of cheaper/more convenient locations

(i) scope for sale and leaseback transactions

15 Weakness of Section 16 Companies Act 1967

There are two weaknesses in Section 16 of the Companies Act 1967 which may be inhibiting its usefulness to shareholders and other users of published accounts. Research is needed into the extent that material divergences between market and book value for properties exist and which are not drawn to the attention of shareholders, but it is disquieting that there appears to be a widespread assumption that such situations are commonplace.* Moreover the Companies Bill 1979 contains nothing to strengthen this Section and the U.K. Government's green paper† states that Article 46.1 of the EEC 4th Directive requires that "the directors' report shall include at least a fair review of the development of the company's business and of its position. It is considered that the requirements expressed in Section 157(1) of the 1948 Act regarding the state of affairs; Section 16 of the 1967 Act regarding the principal activities and any significant change in those activities, significant changes in fixed assets and other matters material for an appreciation of the state of affairs, when taken together, adequately meet the requirements of the Directive."

The first weakness is that there are two hurdles to jump before Section 16 becomes operative. The first, with which no one would quarrel, is that "the market value [must] differ substantially from the [book] amount". The second hurdle is that the "difference is, in the opinion of the directors, of such significance that the attention of the [shareholders or debenture holders] should be drawn thereto". It is generally suspected that there are a large number of differences which would cross the first hurdle but which would fall at the second on such grounds as "it is not the directors' intention to sell the property" or "the properties are fully occupied by the company". Moreover it is at least debatable whether such reasons are adequate for non-disclosure of a material difference.

The second weakness is that Section 16 applies only to the directors' report which is not covered by the auditors' report. Shareholders and other users of accounts do not therefore receive the

* For a description of company practice see p.17 *et seq.* above.

† Company Accounting and Disclosure, Command 7654, HMSO, September 1979, p.33.

protection that an audit requirement would provide by requiring the directors to justify any lack of publication in this area.

Article 51(1)(b) of the EEC Fourth Directive states "The person or persons responsible for auditing the accounts must also verify that the annual report is consistent with the annual accounts for the same financial year". This provision is not likely to increase materially the shareholders' protection in this area, and the U.K. has until 1980 to incorporate the Fourth Directive into its domestic law.

The relevant paragraphs* of the U.K. Government's green paper are as follows:

"In addition to requiring an audit of the annual accounts, Article 51 also requires the auditor to verify that the directors' report is consistent with the annual accounts for the year. This latter requirement will necessitate an extension of the statutory duties of auditors set out in Section 14 of the 1967 Act. It is proposed that, because the nature of the examination and opinion required is different from that applicable to the annual accounts, the auditor should be required to refer to the directors' report in his audit report in order to make clear to readers the limitation of his responsibilities."

"It is considered that the Directive requires the whole content of the directors' report to be scrutinised for consistency by the auditors so that any items which are included, in addition to the minimum requirements of the Directive set out in Article 46, will also be covered. It is proposed that the audit report should refer specifically to the limited nature of the opinion given by the auditor regarding the information included in the directors' report in order that there would be little possibility of anyone being misled as to the degree of confirmation being provided. Any extra-statutory information which the directors may wish to include in their report will be a matter for them to discuss with the auditors in the light of the extended duties of the auditors."

It would seem desirable that any need to remedy the weaknesses in Section 16 should be discussed between the representative bodies of the interested parties, i.e. bodies representing users of accounts, auditors, directors and valuers. The discussions should be expanded to encompass (a) the fact that valuations of property may now be shown in three places (the directors' report, the 'historical cost' accounts, and the current cost accounts) and (b) the desirability of limiting the burden of any additional disclosure on small companies.

* op. cit. p.55.

16 Matching values to users

In Section 2 the users of published accounts were described and in Section 6 the main values that can be provided were described. In this section an attempt is made to bring the two together in order to see which value is most helpful to each of the user groups.

Open market values are probably the most useful values to most users of accounts. Whichever is the higher of the two O.M.V.'s is V_S in terms of Section 11. But users need to know if the alternative use O.M.V. is materially different from the existing use O.M.V. (see also Section 15).

Historical cost is important for stewardship accounting to shareholders and providers of loan capital at the time the property is acquired but its relevance fades as that date recedes into the past. This point applies equally to a valuation. Its relevance also diminishes as the date of the valuation recedes into the past.

Depreciated replacement cost is probably not useful to a lender (e.g. a bank or debenture holder) looking for security for his loan, as it may well be significantly higher than realisable value (V_S).

Undepreciated replacement cost may be useful to management as a guide to how much depreciation to set aside in order to be able eventually to replace the property, or for use in connection with a fire insurance valuation. The difficulty in applying it to replacement is that in many companies the date when it will be necessary to replace its property is a long way off. Directors may well feel that there are so many unquantifiable possible occurrences before replacement day that the depreciation exercise is somewhat artificial and irrelevant to today's more pressing problems.

A going concern value is relevant when the business as a whole may be sold and the property is not valued separately.

Forced sale value is of use to the lender as it is a measure of the value of his security in the unfortunate circumstances in which he would need to call upon it. The extent to which a forced sale value will be less than the open market value will depend on the 'marketability' of the property. This in turn could depend on how specialised the property is. Other factors could include how well served it is by transport, whether it is subject to planning restrictions, how good is the local supply of labour and housing, how convenient it is to customers and suppliers, etc.

Deprival value is likely to be used in the statements to account for inflation on the Current Cost Accounting method.

The effect of CGT and DLT

It is important to remember that if a company sells its property it may be liable to corporation tax on its capital gain. This may mean that the lender stands to receive significantly less than even the forced sale value.

It is not normal for a valuer to make any allowance for capital gains liability to corporation tax or development land tax in his valuation. His valuation is normally the price which would appear on the contract. Directors may need to adjust this price for any taxes, and costs of acquisition or realisation, except in the case of a D.R.C. valuation which will include the cost of creating the asset.

In many cases the absence of any allowance for corporation tax on the capital gain is not important because the proceeds will be used to buy another property, and therefore roll-over relief will be available so that no tax liability will crystallise on the sale. Total exposure to corporation tax should be shown, however, in a note (SSAP 15).

Conclusion

The fact that more than one value is relevant to the users of published accounts suggests that a company's annual report should contain more than one valuation figure provided that each figure was clearly explained.

17 Should the contents of the valuer's report be disclosed?

The valuer submits his report to the directors of the company. The auditor is entitled to see it whether the value is used in the accounts, or only in the directors' report. It is not usual for the content of the valuer's report to be disclosed or made available to anyone other than those commissioning it, although the users of published accounts are to some extent protected from being misled by a recommendation that all valuers' reports should contain the following clause:

Neither the whole nor any part of this Valuation Certificate or any reference thereto may be included in any published document, circular or statement nor published in any way without the Valuer's written approval of the form and context in which it may appear.*

It is normal for a valuer's report to contain a number of caveats and it is at least arguable that the sophisticated user should have access to these caveats in order to interpret properly the valuation figure.

* RICS Guidance Note A2.

Examples of caveats

The following are examples of such caveats drawn from several different valuation reports prepared by Richard Ellis:

(a) No allowance has been made in our valuations for expenses of purchase or realisation, or any liability for Corporation Taxes which may arise on disposal.

(b) Finally, there are one or two properties where the 'existing use value' reflects the special suitability of the properties for their present user. In such cases, we are of the opinion that, because of their special nature, the market for the properties, if they were offered for sale with vacant possession, would be extremely limited and the existing use values might not be realised in such a sale. Where there is a material difference between the existing use value and open market value we will make specific comment in the appropriate Schedules.

(c) Should the Company decide to leave the area completely we are of the opinion that the value of the Main Works with vacant possession is substantially below the existing use value, but with a phased disposal we feel the other properties are capable of being sold at figures in line with those reported, although a fairly long marketing period might be required.

(d) In the current United Kingdom property investment market, there are institutional purchasers for properties of this size where the property is fully let at or near the full market rental value. In this particular instance, as the property is unlet and no income is being received either to cover the interest on the purchase money or to compensate for the lack of interest had the money for the purchase been invested elsewhere, then, any potential purchaser of the building would require a substantial discount on its investment value if completed and let. We have reflected this in our valuation. It could well be that, because the property is unlet, it could take a considerable time for a sale to be effected.

Once the lease has been executed, the property will be leasehold for 99 years and, although the amount of ground rent will be proportionately low, it will be reviewable every year if the rents received by the Company change. Investors are currently looking for freehold properties or leaseholds which have terms of 125 years or more. The relatively short term of the lease particularly would make this building an unattractive investment in the current market, even if it was completed and let.

In our view, the most likely purchaser of this particular property in its existing state would be a fund looking for capital growth as opposed to income, or perhaps another property company which is willing to take on the property with the sale of the resulting investment when the property is fully let. In either case, the number of purchasers in both categories in the current U.K. investment market is strictly limited.

On the information which has been supplied to us by the Company, on the basis that there are no onerous covenants of which we have no knowledge, and on the basis of the contents of this report, it is our opinion that on the open market today, the value of the building, subject to the terms of the Agreement and Head Lease, vacant and unlet is at or about £8 million (eight million pounds sterling).

Similarly, on the same assumptions, but on the basis that the building was completed and fully let, it is our view that the value of the completed investment on the open market today is at or about £11 million (eleven million pounds sterling).

(e) *Condition and repair*
We have not undertaken a structural survey of any of the buildings, nor arranged for tests or inspections to be carried out on any of the service installations. Our valuations have been prepared on the basis that the properties are in a satisfactory state of repair and condition, and that High Alumina Cement concrete, Woodwool slabs, or Blue Asbestos have not been used in the construction of the buildings.

(f) Both properties lie within a Development Area with the availability of building grants of up to 20% in respect of new construction, together with allied tax concessions. In general terms, this means that almost 50% of the cost of a new factory is met through grants or allowances, but the same incentives are not available to purchasers of existing industrial premises. As a result, prospective purchasers of existing factories tend to have regard to the net cost of the alternative of acquiring new premises and we have reflected this factor in arriving at our opinions of value.

(g) We would point out that our valuations take no account of any grants that might be available, where appropriate, under the Redmeat Slaughterhouse Industry Scheme (as set up under Section 8 of the Industry Act 1972) or from the European Economic Community Agricultural Fund (F.E.O.G.A.).

Relevant Parts of Valuer's Report to be made available to users of accounts

These examples show how a valuation whilst being 'the truth' is not necessarily 'the whole truth' and the importance of the user seeing the valuer's report and not just the resulting figure. A major lender can no doubt insist on seeing the report, and would be well advised to do so, but other users are at present denied what could be important information. It is suggested therefore that directors should be encouraged by whatever means are appropriate to make the relevant parts of the valuer's report available to all users of accounts.

Care would have to be taken that a company's competitive position was not weakened by the publication of the valuer's report. For example, the report might indicate the rent the company expected to get from a tenant at the next rent review, and this might hamper negotiations with the tenant, or it might indicate a policy of acquiring land bit by bit in a particular area and this could weaken its bargaining position for remaining key sites.

A way of countering this difficulty would be for the valuer to provide a short form report, for publication, containing all the caveats which he considers to be material.

These suggestions, and the nature of suitable safeguards to a company's competitive position, would need to be considered by such bodies as the Society of Investment Analysts, The Stock Exchange, CBI, The Institute of Directors, The Institute of Chartered Accountants in England and Wales and other members of the Consultative Committee of Accounting Bodies, the Royal Institution of Chartered Surveyors, and the Department of Trade.

A convenient mechanism for making the report available while keeping cost to a minimum would be for it to be attached to the annual report placed at the Companies Registry.

Auditors', directors' and valuers' responsibility to the users of accounts

Meanwhile it is important for a company's auditors to study the valuer's report to assure themselves that any use of the valuation in the accounts contributes to a 'true and fair view' in the light of any caveats or other comments in the valuer's report. In addition, it would be helpful for the auditor to be present at the meeting between the directors and the valuers at which their instructions are agreed, so that all three parties could be agreed at the outset as to what information is needed from the valuer and from the directors, and what will need to be included in the directors' report and accounts in order to give a true and fair view.

The prime legal responsibility for the directors' report and the accounts is the directors', but the auditor and valuer also have inescapable professional responsibilities.

After studying the valuers' report the auditor might conclude, in certain circumstances, that in order to give a true and fair view, it was necessary to include in the notes to the accounts, not the whole of the valuer's report, but some of the 'ifs' and 'buts' similar to those quoted earlier in this Section.

The valuer should consider, when asked for his consent to include his valuation figure, or one of his valuation figures, in a company's annual report, whether showing the figure(s) by themselves might be potentially misleading. If there is such a danger he should withhold his consent until the bare figures have been appropriately amplified or qualified.

18 Goodwill

It has already been noted (in Section 5 above) that for certain types of property (e.g. hotels and cinemas) it is difficult to value the property separately from the business carried on in it. This means that the property valuation will include an element of 'goodwill'.

Again we have seen that a D.R.C. valuation may be reduced because of inadequate profitability (R.I.C.S. Guidance Note A2(2)(iv)). Such a reduction might be described as 'negative goodwill'.

The user of accounts needs to be cautious when either of these situations occurs. The first will tend to lead to lower rates of return on capital than would otherwise be obtained. It also means that rates of return from such companies cannot be compared with other companies which have followed the normal process of not capitalising internally generated goodwill.

In the second situation, return on capital will be as high as the directors' concept of 'adequate profitability'.

In neither situation is return on capital a reliable or comparable measure of the efficiency of the directors (and see page 5 above). Unfortunately it would appear that only rarely will the user be provided with the information necessary for him to be aware that these situations exist.

Incidentally the EEC 4th Directive (Article 37.2) may require goodwill to be written off within a maximum period of 5 years, which is considerably faster than it is normal to depreciate property. Member states may, however, permit companies to write goodwill off systematically over a limited period exceeding five years provided that this period does not exceed the useful economic life of the asset and is disclosed in the notes on the accounts together with the supporting reasons therefore.

The U.K. Government's green paper says "it is intended to take advantage of this derogation and in doing so to leave it to companies to assess the economic life of goodwill in their individual circumstances. It is for consideration whether it would be appropriate for the law to stipulate a maximum period for the writing off of goodwill, say 20 or 40 years."*

* op. cit. p.38.

VI

Conclusions and recommendations

1   There is a problem of communication between valuers, accountants, auditors, directors, and users of accounts on the subject of the valuation and depreciation of property. It is hoped that this book will help to improve the degree of understanding between the various parties concerned.

2   Whilst all conventions are artificial, accountants and valuers need to be aware of the *degree* of artificiality of the conventions necessarily adopted by each other.

3   Because accounts are produced for a variety of users, they may well fail to provide all the information needed by any one group of users.

4   Because of the combination of the relatively long life of property, general inflation, and the movement in the specific prices of a company's property, the relevance and usefulness to the various users of published accounts of the historical cost of the property declines over time. There is a need therefore to provide up-to-date values.

5   It is debatable whether such up-to-date values are better incorporated in the balance sheet or in a note to the accounts. The volatility of property prices and the artificiality of some valuations are arguments in favour of using the notes to the accounts. This would leave the basic accounts prepared purely on the historical cost convention and not a mixture of historical costs and current values. Current values would appear in the notes to the historical cost accounts and in the current cost accounts.

81

6   It is desirable that the value of property should be sub-divided in the notes to the accounts into the same groups as are currently required by the Stock Exchange for prospectuses, i.e.:

(a) held as investments
(b) being developed
(c) held for development in the future
(d) held for disposal
(e) owner occupied*

7   Although there are many values which can be ascribed to a property there are only two which need to be considered in most circumstances. They are O.M.V. 'for existing use' and O.M.V. for 'alternative use'. O.M.V. for existing use can be either arrived at by comparison with similar properties or, in the absence of such evidence, by D.R.C., but in the latter case always subject to a caveat concerning adequate profitability. Ideally a balance sheet valuation should probably be an O.M.V. 'for existing use' based on a comparison with similar properties, but where this is not possible D.R.C. must be used. Because there is less external evidence for a D.R.C. valuation than for an O.M. valuation, one of the notes to the accounts should indicate how much of a valuation is made up of O.M.V. and how much is D.R.C. If the D.R.C. has been reduced because of lack of adequate profitability, then that fact should be stated, the amount of the reduction quantified, and the directors' definition of 'adequate profitability' explained.

8   It would be desirable for the R.I.C.S. to clarify the distinction between:

(a) open market value for existing *use*
(b) open market value to the existing *user*.

9   Directors should give the basis of valuation of property more frequently than at present. Directors and valuers should be encouraged to use a more standardised description of the basis of valuation than is current practice.

---

* Property let to an employee under a service tenancy should be treated as operational property, owner-occupied by the company, and valued at its O.M.V. with vacant possession.

10 Where it has been necessary to apportion an O.M.V. between a 'building' and a 'land' element in order to calculate depreciation then the method of apportionment used should be disclosed in the notes to the accounts if the figure is material.

11 Where it has been necessary to apportion an O.M.V. of a leasehold to arrive at a depreciable amount, the relevant facts should be given in a note to the accounts.

12 If D.R.C. exceeds O.M.V. and depreciation is based on the O.M.V. then this fact and the relevant figures should be disclosed in a note to the accounts.

13 The R.I.C.S. and A.S.C. should express a preference for one of the two methods currently recommended for the apportionment of an O.M.V. between 'land' and 'buildings'.
   If depreciation is regarded as an allocation of the cost of, or a valuation of, the property to the time periods which have benefited from its use then method (a) (i.e. deducting the value of the land from the value of the property) should be preferred. If depreciation is regarded as a mechanism by means of which funds are retained to finance the eventual replacement of the property then method (b) (i.e. assessing the net replacement cost of the buildings) should be preferred.

14 It would be a considerable simplification, and save time and money, if no apportionment between 'land' and 'buildings' were to be required, and depreciation was to be calculated on the total value of the property, where depreciation so calculated would not have a material effect on the profit figure. Whilst this would be theoretically incorrect if it is assumed that land does not depreciate, the resulting 'error' could well be less than the potential 'error' in (a) valuing the property and (b) apportioning the value between 'land' and 'buildings'.

15 If the O.M.V. (i.e. what the property could be sold for) is materially different (either *lower* or higher) from the existing use value then the extent of the difference should be reported. Further research into the adequacy of the working of Section 16 of the Companies Act 1967 is needed and in the light of the results of such research it may be desirable to improve the wording of that section.

16   It would be reasonable to qualify an alternative use value with a description of, and possibly some quantification of, the costs both direct and indirect which a move from the present premises would involve.

17   Where the O.M.V. for existing use has been arrived at by reducing a D.R.C. valuation for inadequate profitability, that fact should be disclosed and the reduction quantified.

18   An auditor should if possible attend the meeting at which the directors agree the valuer's instructions. Auditors should study carefully the valuer's report to see whether any parts of it need to be included in the notes to the accounts in order that any accounts including a valuation show a true and fair view. Valuers should withhold their consent to publish their valuation figure(s) unless the figure(s) have been appropriately amplified or qualified in words which are clear to the users of accounts.

19   The desirability of (a) the valuer producing a short form report, including all material caveats, for publication, or (b) the full valuer's report being made available to users of accounts by being filed at the Companies Registry needs to be considered by the relevant bodies.

20   Users, preparers and auditors of accounts and valuers need to be alert to possible misunderstandings between them over such matters as plant, repairs, interim valuations, capital gains charge to corporation tax, development land tax, grants and goodwill.

Bibliography

Accounting Standards 1979, Institute of Chartered Accountants in England and Wales, 1979

Admission of Securities to Listing, Stock Exchange

ATTWOOD, F.A., *Companies Accounts Checklist*, Institute of Chartered Accountants in England and Wales, 1979

BAXTER, W.T., *Depreciation*, Sweet and Maxwell, 1971

BEAN AND LOCKWOOD, *Rating Valuation Practice*, 6th Edition, J.C. Bassett and C. Wheeler, Stevens, 1969

BONBRIGHT, J.C., *The valuation of property*, The Michie Company, 1937

CLEMENS, J.H. AND DYER, L.S., *Balance Sheets and the Lending Banker*, Europa Publications, 5th Edition, 1977

Company Accounting and Disclosure, Command 7654, HMSO, 1979

Companies Act 1967, HMSO

Corporate Report, Accounting Standards Steering Committee, 1975

GRAHAM, B., DODD, D.L., COTTLE, S., *Security Analysis: Principles and Technique*, McGraw Hill, 1962

LEE, T.A., AND TWEEDIE, D.P., *The Private Shareholder and the Corporate Report*, Institute of Chartered Accountants in England and Wales, 1977

MILNES, A, and TILLETT, D. *Property Company Accounts*, Institute of Chartered Accountants in England and Wales, 1978.

NOKE, C., "The reality of property depreciation", *Accountancy*, November and December 1979

RENWICK, F.B., *Introduction to Investment and Finance*, Macmillan, 1971

Royal Institution of Chartered Surveyors, *Guidance Notes on the Valuation of Assets*

Survey of Published Accounts, 1978, Institute of Chartered Accountants in England and Wales, 1979

TURVEY, R., *The Economics of Real Property*, Allen and Unwin, 1957

WATTS, T.R. (Ed.), *Handbook on the EEC Fourth Directive*, Institute of Chartered Accountants in England and Wales, 1979

WEAVER, D., *Investment Analysis*, Longmans, 1971

WOOLEY, A., *The Art of Valuation*, Lexington Books, 1978

Appendix 1

Valuations of company property assets and their disclosure in directors' reports or accounts or companies

This Statement S.20 was issued in February 1974 by the Institute of Chartered Accountants in England and Wales to their members at the same time as Guidance Note No. A.2 was issued by the RICS.

Revaluations of company property assets are frequently undertaken and are often incorporated in the accounts of companies in the United Kingdom. Where the revaluation is not incorporated in the accounts it is nevertheless usual to disclose it in the directors' report or Chairman's statement. Moreover, Section 16(i) (a) of the Companies Act 1967 requires the difference between the market value of property assets and the balance sheet amount to be disclosed in the directors' report if, in the opinion of the directors, it is significant.

Introduction

1   Valuations, as with other exercises in the use of judgement, depend very largely on the assumptions and bases that are used in making them. It is well known that a valuation for one purpose, such as insurance, may well be entirely different from a valuation for another purpose, such as a forced sale. It is important, therefore, that in any disclosure relating to a valuation, the basis of the valuation should be clearly stated. The disclosure of the basis used, when alternatives are acceptable, is a recognised feature of accounting practices.

2   Hitherto it has not been common practice for companies to state in adequate detail the basis of valuation of property assets in accounts for directors' reports, and this has sometimes created difficulties. It could in certain circumstances even be misleading. The Council has therefore decided to issue the following guidance to members on this matter.

Bases of Valuation

3   Various bases of valuation are in common use such as, 'current open market', 'existing use', 'alternative use', 'depreciated replacement cost', 'going concern', etc. Some of these are suitable for use when the valuation is to be incorporated in the accounts of a company, others when merely disclosure is made in the directors' report or chairman's statement.

Some like 'going concern', are regarded as unsuitable for use in relation to property assets of a company.

4   The acceptable bases, the circumstances in which they should be used and suggestions concerning the frequency of valuations are set out in Guidance Notes which have been issued by the Royal Institution of Chartered Surveyors to its members. The Guidance Notes were prepared by a joint working party consisting of members of the Institute of Chartered Accountants in England and Wales and of the Royal Institution of Chartered Surveyors. Members should use their best endeavours to ensure, in relation to the accounts or directors' reports of companies with which they are concerned, that these principles are observed.

Other Matters

5   Guidance on when it is appropriate to include property valuations in the balance sheet as opposed to disclosing them by way of note and questions concerning accounting treatments resulting from the inclusion of valuations in accounts are technical matters requiring separate considerations and are therefore not dealt with in this statement. Such matters, some of which are already under consideration for inclusion in Statements of Standard Accounting Practice, include the treatment and disclosure of resulting revaluation surpluses or deficits, the treatment of tax liabilities which would accrue if the asset were disposed of at its revalued figure, and the depreciation policy following a revaluation.

6   In accordance with normal accounting practice, the valuation of any properties held as trading stock should not be incorporated in the accounts if it is above cost.

Appendix 2

Valuation of company property assets

**Principles to be observed when Valuations are
to be incorporated in Company Accounts or Directors' Reports**

1. The Institution issued these Guidance Notes to members on certain aspects of the valuation of company property assets in order to implement the conclusions agreed between the Institution and the Institute of Chartered Accountants in England and Wales following the report of a joint Working Party, set up in 1973, on the subject.

2. Members are recommended to take particular note of the following and to adopt the procedures in all appropriate cases:–

Basis of Valuation

(i) Any valuation of land and buildings has regard to evidence of current open market transactions in similar property. Such valuations may reflect either:–

    (a) the use of the property for the same purpose as hitherto ('existing use valuation'); or

    (b) the prospective use of the property for some other purpose ('alternative use valuation').

The market value under (a) above may include a special element attributable to the earning potential of the premises for a particular existing purpose by reason of their nature, location and character. Such element of value (if present) subsists irrespective of the benefit of the property to the particular undertaking of which it forms a part.

(ii) Open market value as described above may, for a variety of reasons, be higher or lower than 'depreciated replacement cost' namely the current cost of acquiring the site and erecting the premises less an appropriate deduction for their present condition.

(iii) Because the value of a business as a going concern must take account of intangibles (particularly goodwill) and reflect overall earning capacity, such value cannot be properly apportioned to any particular property assets of the entity, except to the extent that the special element of value enters into the open market value as in (i)(a) above. It follows therefore that the expression 'going concern valuation' in relation to company property should not be used.

All property valuations for disclosure in directors' reports or accounts should only be on the basis set out in sub-paragraph (i) or in appropriate cases (described in sub-paragraph (iv)) on the basis of depreciated replacement cost as defined in sub-paragraph (ii).

88

Since a company's property assets may have two or more possibly differing market values, where it is evident that the difference is material the Valuer should quote figures of both existing use value (sub-paragraph (i) (a)) and alternative use value (sub-paragraph (i) (b)).

(iv) There are some kinds of property which are rarely (if ever) sold except by way of sale of the business as a whole. Examples are oil refineries, chemical works, quarries with lime kilns, factories which are no more than cladding to a specialist plant, and, perhaps, factories located in a remote area for particular reasons. In these special cases an existing use valuation can only be made by reference to the depreciated replacement cost as described in sub-paragraph (ii) and such valuation should be expressed as subject to adequate profitability related to the value of the total assets.

Valuations to be incorporated in accounts or in notes thereto

(v) For property assets used for the purposes of a business, only existing use valuations as in (i) (a) above or where appropriate the depreciated replacement cost as in sub-paragraph (ii) are suitable to be incorporated in the accounts because basic accounting concepts postulate that the accounts are on a going concern basis; that is to say, that the enterprise will continue in operational existence for the foreseeable future and in particular that the profit and loss account and balance sheet assume no intention nor necessity to liquidate or curtail significantly the scale of operation. In this context the alternative use value as in sub-paragraph (i) (b) of assets without which the business could not function, has no relevance. Such value may, however, be relevant to an overall appraisal of the company's situation and where significant should be disclosed in the directors' report, as envisaged by Section 16(i) (a) of the Companies Act 1967.

Companies other than Property Companies

(vi) Where the potential surplus or deficit on a valuation of a company's property assets compared with the amount at which they are shown in the accounts is material in relation to net assets, the directors should consider the advisability of having independent valuations carried out regularly and preferably at intervals of three to five years. Such valuations, if not incorporated in the accounts, should be disclosed in the directors' report in compliance with Section 16(i) (a) of the Companies Act 1967. In the intervening years, the latest valuation should be referred to in the directors' report, with an expression of opinion by the directors whether there has been a material increase or decrease in value since the date of that valuation. Valuations of company property assets should include all leasehold interests whether or not a premium was paid on their acquisition.

Property Companies

(vii) The general principles concerning valuations of a company's property assets set out above will also apply to property companies. There will generally, however, be a need for more frequent valuations and the directors should, therefore, consider the advisability of obtaining independent valuations annually. Such valuations, which should cover all properties, should be under the following headings which include the requirements of the Stock Exchange publication ADMISSION OF SECURITIES TO LISTING:

(a) Properties occupied primarily by the company

(b) Properties held as investments

(c) Properties being developed

(d) Properties held for development in the future

(e) Properties held for disposal.

If any such valuation is to be incorporated in the accounts of a company, property being developed or which is not fully let should be valued at its realisable value in its existing state at the date of the valuation.

89

Valuation Certificate Procedures

(viii) The following procedures apply to Valuation Certificates for both non-property and property companies:–

    (a) the basis and date of valuation must be clearly stated;

    (b) the name, address and qualifications of the valuer must be given with the date of his certificate;

    (c) all material factors used in the valuation, e.g. assumptions about planning permissions not yet obtained, must be stated;

    (d) separate valuation totals for freehold and leasehold properties must be given;

    (e) the valuation format in reporting to a Company for use in a financial statement for the Company's accounts should follow the specimen valuation format[1] in the Stock Exchange book ADMISSION OF SECURITIES TO LISTING with the addition of headings (a) and (e) of sub-paragraph (vii) above where appropriate.

Valuer's Letter of Consent

(ix) The Valuer's certificate should state that his written consent to any reference to his valuation in company accounts and/or directors' reports or any company statement or circular must be obtained before such documents are published. All Valuation Certificates should therefore incorporate a paragraph to the effect that:–

> 'Neither the whole nor any part of this Valuation Certificate or any reference thereto may be included in any published document, circular or statement nor published in any way without the Valuer's written approval of the form and context in which it may appear'.

3. It is to be particularly noted that the concept of a 'going concern value' is now dropped and alternative approaches are set out.

4. The Valuer's letter of consent as referred to in paragraph 2 (ix) above should only be given when a final proof of the document, etc., is available and the consent should refer to a specimen annexed and signed as identification of what has been approved. It should be made clear to the client when instructions are taken that the valuer's consent must be obtained prior to each and every publication of the whole or part of the valuation certificate including references to it in company accounts and/or directors' reports of any company statement or circular.

5. It is essential that the requirements of the Stock Exchange and the City Panel on Take-Overs and Mergers be observed as otherwise the interest of the client may be jeopardised.

6. Members are advised to discuss and agree with the client the actual basis of valuation; it is helpful if in this connection the client will disclose the purpose of the valuation. This is particularly important in those cases where a property portfolio is being divided between more than one valuer. Care should be taken in using correctly such bases as 'open market value', 'fair market value' and 'fair market value as between a willing seller and a willing buyer'[2].

7. The attention of members is drawn to the Guidance Notes[3] published in the CHARTERED SURVEYOR for June 1973, which should be read in conjunction with these Notes.

8. The Institution is setting up a Standing Committee[4] whose responsibility will be to scrutinise all published valuations and references which have given or could give rise to concern. In such an event this Committee would seek to discuss with the member concerned the reasons underlying any departure from this or any other Guidance Note.

[1] A suitable format is to be found immediately following this Guidance Note.

[2] The Institution has since recommended that 'open market value' only be used. See Guidance Note No. A.3. paras 3 and 6.

[3] Guidance note No. A.1 entitled 'Valuation of Company Property Assets (Information in Prospectuses and Circulars).

[4] The Assets Valuation Standards Committee has this duty within its terms of reference.

(First published February 1974)

Appendix 3

Statements of standard accounting practice

2. Disclosure of accounting policies *(Issued November 1971)*
© The Institute of Chartered Accountants in England and Wales.

It is fundamental to the understanding and interpretation of financial accounts that those who use them should be aware of the main assumptions on which they are based. The purpose of the Statement which follows is to assist such understanding by promoting improvement in the quality of information disclosed. It seeks to achieve this by establishing as standard accounting practice the disclosure in financial accounts of clear explanations of the accounting policies followed in so far as these are significant for the purpose of giving a true and fair view. The Statement does not seek to establish accounting standards for individual items; these will be dealt with in separate Statements of Standard Accounting Practice issued from time to time.

PART 1 – EXPLANATORY NOTE
**Fundamental accounting concepts,
accounting bases and accounting policies**
In accounting usage terms such as 'accounting principles', 'practices', 'rules', 'conventions', 'methods' or 'procedures' have often been treated as interchangeable.*[1] For the purpose of this Statement it is convenient to distinguish between *fundamental accounting concepts, accounting bases* and *accounting policies*.

Fundamental accounting concepts are here defined as broad basic assumptions which underlie the periodic financial accounts of business enterprises. It is expedient to single out for special mention four in particular: (a) the 'going concern' concept (b) the 'accruals' concept (c) the 'consistency' concept and (d) the 'prudence' concept.*[2] The use of these concepts is not necessarily self-evident from an examination of accounts, but they have such general acceptance that they call for

*[1] In this series 'accounting practices' has been adopted as a generic term to encompass all aspects of financial accounting methods and presentation.

*[2] It is emphasised that it is not the purpose of this Statement to develop a basic theory of accounting. An exhaustive theoretical approach would take an entirely different form and would include, for instance, many more propositions than the four fundamental concepts referred to here. It is, however, expedient to recognise them as working assumptions having general acceptance at the present time.

92

no explanation in published accounts and their observance is presumed unless stated otherwise. They are practical rules rather than theoretical ideals and are capable of variation and evolution as accounting thought and practice develop, but their present generally accepted meanings are restated in paragraph 14 below.

Accounting bases are the methods which have been developed for expressing or applying fundamental accounting concepts to financial transactions and items. By their nature accounting bases are more diverse and numerous than fundamental concepts, since they have evolved in response to the variety and complexity of types of business and business transactions, and for this reason there may justifiably exist more than one recognised accounting basis for dealing with particular items. 3

Accounting policies are the specific accounting bases judged by business enterprises to be most appropriate to their circumstances and adopted by them for the purpose of preparing their financial accounts. 4

Particular problems in application of the fundamental concepts

The main difficulty in applying the fundamental accounting concepts arises from the fact that many business transactions have financial effects spreading over a number of years. Decisions have to be made on the extent to which expenditure incurred in one year can reasonably be expected to produce benefits in the form of revenue in other years and should therefore be carried forward, in whole or in part; that is, should be dealt with in the closing balance sheet, as distinct from being dealt with as an expense of the current year in the profit and loss account because the benefit has been exhausted in that year. 5

In some cases revenue is received for goods or services the production or supply of which will involve some later expenditure. In this case a decision must be made regarding how much of the revenue should be carried forward, to be dealt with in subsequent profit and loss accounts when the relevant costs are incurred. 6

All such decisions require consideration of future events of uncertain financial effect, and to this extent an element of commercial judgement is unavoidable in the assessment. 7

Examples of matters which give rise to particular difficulty are: the future benefits to be derived from stocks and all types of work in progress at the end of the year; the future benefits to be derived from fixed assets, and the period of years over which these will be fruitful; the extent to which expenditure on research and development can be expected to produce future benefits. 8

Purpose and limitations of accounting bases

In the course of practice there have developed a variety of accounting bases designed to provide consistent, fair and as nearly as possible objective solutions to these problems in particular circumstances; for instance bases for calculating such items as depreciation, the amounts at which stocks and work in progress are to be stated, and deferred taxation. 9

Accounting bases provide an orderly and consistent framework for periodic reporting of a concern's results and financial position, but they do not, and are not intended to, substitute for the exercise of commercial judgement in the preparation of financial reports. Where a choice of acceptable accounting bases is available judgement must be exercised in choosing those which are appropriate to the circumstances and are best suited to present fairly the concern's results and financial position; the bases thus adopted then become the concern's accounting policies. The significance of accounting bases is that they provide limits to the area subject to the exercise of judgement, and a check against arbitrary, excessive or unjustifiable adjustments where no other objective yardstick is available. By definition it is not possible to develop generalised rules for the exercise of judgement, though practical working rules may be evolved on a pragmatic basis for limited use in particular circumstances. Broadly, the longer a concern's normal business cycle – the period between initiation of business transactions and their completion – the greater the area subject to judgement and its effect on periodic financial accounts, and the less its susceptibility to close regulation by accounting bases. These limitations to the regulating powers of accounting bases must be recognised.

Significance of disclosure of accounting policies
In circumstances where more than one accounting basis is acceptable in principle, the accounting policy followed can significantly affect a concern's reported results and financial position and the view presented can be properly appreciated only if the policies followed in dealing with material items are also explained. For this reason adequate disclosure of the accounting policies is essential to the fair presentation of financial accounts. As accounting standards become established through publication of Statements of Standard Accounting Practice, the choice of accounting bases regarded as generally available will diminish, but it has to be recognised that the complexity and diversity of business renders total and rigid uniformity of bases impracticable.

The items with which this Statement is mainly concerned are those which are subject to the exercise of judgement as to how far they should be dealt with in the profit and loss account for the period under review or how far all or part should be carried forward in the balance sheet as attributable to the operations of future periods. The determination of the annual profit or loss of nearly every business substantially depends on a systematic approach to a few material items of this type. For the better appreciation of the view they give, annual accounts should include a clear explanation of the accounting policies followed for dealing with these few key items (some examples of which are given in paragraph 13 below). The intention and spirit of this Statement are that management should identify those items of the type described which are judged material or critical for the purpose of determining and fully appreciating the company's profit or loss and its financial position, and should make clear the accounting policies followed for dealing with them.

Examples of matters for which different accounting bases are recognised
Significant matters for which different accounting bases are recognised and which may have a material effect on reported results and financial position include:

— depreciation of fixed assets
— treatment and amortisation of intangibles such as research and development expenditure, patents and trademarks

- stocks and work in progress
- long-term contracts
- deferred taxation
- hire-purchase or instalment transactions
- leasing and rental transactions
- conversion of foreign currencies
- repairs and renewals
- consolidation policies
- property development transactions
- warranties for products or services.

This list is not exhaustive, and may vary according to the nature of the operations conducted.

PART 2 – DEFINITION OF TERMS

Fundamental accounting concepts are the broad basic assumptions which underlie the periodic financial accounts of business enterprises. At the present time the four following fundamental concepts (the relative importance of which will vary according to the circumstances of the particular case) are regarded as having general acceptability: 14

(a) the 'going concern' concept: the enterprise will continue in operational existence for the foreseeable future. This means in particular that the profit and loss account and balance sheet assume no intention or necessity to liquidate or curtail significantly the scale of operation;

(b) the 'accruals' concept: revenue and costs are accrued (that is, recognised as they are earned or incurred, not as money is received or paid), matched with one another so far as their relationship can be established or justifiably assumed, and dealt with in the profit and loss account of the period to which they relate; provided that where the accruals concept is inconsistent with the 'prudence' concept (paragraph (d) below), the latter prevails. The accruals concept implies that the profit and loss account reflects changes in the amount of net assets that arise out of the transactions of the relevant period (other than distributions or subscriptions of capital and unrealised surpluses arising on revaluation of fixed assets). Revenue and profits dealt with in the profit and loss account are matched with associated costs and expenses by including in the same account the costs incurred in earning them (so far as these are material and identifiable);

(c) the 'consistency' concept: there is consistency of accounting treatment of like items within each accounting period and from one period to the next;

(d) the concept of 'prudence': revenue and profits are not anticipated, but are recognised by inclusion in the profit and loss account only when realised in the form either of cash or of other assets the ultimate cash realisation of which can be assessed with reasonable certainty; provision is made for all known liabilities (expenses and losses) whether the amount of these is known with certainty or is a best estimate in the light of the information available.

Accounting bases are the methods developed for applying fundamental accounting concepts to financial transactions and items, for the purpose of financial accounts, and in particular (a) for determining the accounting periods in which revenue and costs should be recognised in the profit and loss account and (b) for determining the amounts at which material items should be stated in the balance sheet.   15

Accounting policies are the specific accounting bases selected and consistently followed by a business enterprise as being, in the opinion of the management, appropriate to its circumstances and best suited to present fairly its results and financial position.

PART 3 – STANDARD ACCOUNTING PRACTICE

Disclosure of adoption of concepts which differ from those generally accepted

If accounts are prepared on the basis of assumptions which differ in material respects from any of the generally accepted fundamental concepts defined in paragraph 14 above, the facts should be explained. In the absence of a clear statement to the contrary, there is a presumption that the four fundamental concepts have been observed.

Disclosure of accounting policies

The accounting policies (as defined in paragraph 16 above) followed for dealing with items which are judged material or critical in determining profit or loss for the year and in stating the financial position should be disclosed by way of note to the accounts. The explanations should be clear, fair, and as brief as possible.

Date from which effective

The accounting practices set out in this statement should be adopted as soon as possible and regarded as standard in respect of reports relating to accounting periods starting on or after 1st January, 1972.

Appendix 4

Statements of standard accounting practice

12. Accounting for depreciation

© 1977 The Institute of Chartered Accountants in England and Wales.

PART 1 - EXPLANATORY NOTE

Depreciation is a measure of the wearing out, consumption or other loss of value of a fixed asset whether arising from use, effluxion of time or obsolescence through technology and market changes. Depreciation should be allocated to accounting periods so as to charge a fair proportion to each accounting period during the expected useful life of the asset. Depreciation includes amortisation of fixed assets whose useful life is pre-determined (e.g. leases) and depletion of wasting assets (e.g. mines).   1

Assessment of depreciation, and its allocation to accounting periods, involves in the first instance consideration of three factors: 2

(a) cost (or valuation when an asset has been revalued in the financial statements);

(b) the nature of the asset and the length of its expected useful life to the business having due regard to the incidence of obsolescence;

(c) estimated residual value.

An asset's useful life may be: 3

(a) pre-determined, as in leaseholds;

(b) directly governed by extraction or consumption;

(c) dependent on the extent of use;

(d) reduced by obsolescence or physical deterioration.

97

The precise assessment of residual value is normally a difficult matter. Where it is likely to be small in relation to cost, it is convenient to regard it as 'nil' and to deal with any proceeds on eventual disposal in the same way as depreciation over-provided on disposal as referred to in paragraph 6 below.

4

The allocation of depreciation to accounting periods involves the exercise of judgement by management in the light of technical, commercial and accounting considerations and accordingly requires annual review. When, as the result of experience or of changed circumstances, it is considered that the original estimate of useful life of an asset requires to be revised, the unamortised cost of the asset should be charged to revenue over the revised remaining useful life. If at any time the unamortised cost is seen to be irrecoverable in full (perhaps as a result of obsolescence or a fall in demand for a product), it should be written down immediately to the estimated recoverable amount which should be charged over the remaining useful life.

5

Where fixed assets are disposed of for an amount which is greater or less than their book value, the surplus or deficiency should be reflected in the results of the year and disclosed separately if material.

6

The management of a business has a duty to allocate depreciation as fairly as possible to the periods expected to benefit from the use of the asset and should select the method regarded as most appropriate to the type of asset and its use in the business.

7

A change from one method of providing depreciation to another is permissible only on the grounds that the new method will give a fairer presentation of the results and of the financial position. In these circumstances the unamortised cost should be written off over the remaining useful life commencing with the period in which the change is made.

8

Where assets are revalued and effect is given to the revaluation in the financial statements, the charge for depreciation thereafter should be based on the revalued amount and, in the year of change, there should be disclosed by way of note to the financial statements the subdivision of the charge between that applicable to original cost (or valuation if previously revalued) and that applicable to the change in value on the current revaluation, if material.

9

It is not appropriate to omit charging depreciation of a fixed asset on the grounds that its market value is greater than its net book value. If account is taken of such increased value by writing up the net book value of a fixed asset then, as indicated in paragraph 9, an increased charge for depreciation will become necessary.

10

Freehold land, unless subject to depletion by, for example, the extraction of minerals or to reduction in value due to other circumstances, will not normally require a provision for depreciation. However, the value of freehold land may be adversely affected by considerations such as the desirability of its location either socially or in relation to available sources of materials, labour or sales and in these circumstances it should be written down.

11

Buildings have a limited life which may be materially affected by technological and environmental changes and they should be depreciated having regard to the same criteria as in the case of other fixed assets. 12

As in the case of other assets an increase in the value of land or buildings does not remove the necessity for charging depreciation on the buildings whenever any of the causes mentioned in paragraph 1 are applicable, whether or not the value of the asset has increased in the past. 13

Transitional arrangements

Where existing buildings are depreciated for the first time under the terms of this standard it will represent a change in accounting policy and therefore the amount of depreciation charged which relates to prior years should properly be treated as a prior year adjustment and charged against the opening balance of retained profits. 14

PART 2 - DEFINITION OF TERMS

The following definition is used for the purpose of this statement: *Depreciation* is the measure of the wearing out, consumption or other loss of value of a fixed asset whether arising from use, effluxion of time or obsolescence through technology and market changes. 15

PART 3 - STANDARD ACCOUNTING PRACTICE

Accounting treatment

Provision for depreciation of fixed assets having a finite useful life should be made by allocating the cost (or revalued amount) less estimated residual values of the assets as fairly as possible to the periods expected to benefit from their use. 16

Where there is a revision of the estimated useful life of an asset, the unamortised cost should be charged over the revised remaining useful life. 17

However, if at any time the unamortised cost of an asset is seen to be irrecoverable in full, it should be written down immediately to the estimated recoverable amount which should be charged over the remaining useful life. 18

Where there is a change from one method of depreciation to another, the unamortised cost of the asset should be written off over the remaining useful life on the new basis commencing with the period in which the change is made. The effect should be disclosed in the year of change, if material. 19

Where assets are revalued in the financial statements, the provision for depreciation should be based on the revalued amount and current estimate of remaining useful life, with disclosure in the year of change, of the effect of the revaluation, if material. 20

Disclosure

The following should be disclosed in the financial statements for each major class of depreciable asset: 21

99

(a) the depreciation methods used;

(b) the useful lives or the depreciation rates used;

(c) total depreciation allocated for the period;

(d) the gross amount of depreciable assets and the related accumulated depreciation.

Date from which effective

The accounting and disclosure requirements set out in this statement should be adopted as soon as possible and regarded as standard in respect of financial statements relating to periods starting on or after 1st January 1978, except that the provisions of the standard need not be applied to investment properties in respect of periods starting before 1st January 1980.

PART 4 - COMPLIANCE WITH INTERNATIONAL STANDARD NO. 4 'DEPRECIATION ACCOUNTING'

Compliance with the requirements of Statement of Standard Accounting Practice No. 12 ACCOUNTING FOR DEPRECIATION will automatically ensure compliance with International Accounting Standard No. 4 DEPRECIATION ACCOUNTING.

Appendix 5

Guidance notes on the valuation of plant and machinery

For the purpose of incorporating or referring to such value in company accounts, directors' reports and other published financial statements

General

1. The Companies Act 1967 requires that assets shall be classified in the balance sheet under headings appropriate to the company's business and further that fixed assets, current assets and assets that are neither fixed nor current be separately identified but the Act contains no definitions of these classes of assets, although it refers to investments, goodwill, patents and trademarks in terms which recognise the possibility that such assets may be so classified. It should be noted that the very word 'fixed' is somewhat of a misnomer; ships, motor vehicles, railway engines and heavy movable equipment including cranes will be included although some may be classified as 'neither fixed nor current'. Smaller items of plant and machinery, particularly where they are movable, are often classified, for accounting purposes, as neither fixed nor current.

As a matter of practicality, many companies use a minimum expenditure level to account for capital expenditure; thus any item costing less than a specified amount is written off to revenue in the year of purchase whereas strictly speaking such expenditure could be charged to a fixed asset account.

2. Current assets (which will include stocks and work in progress) are in general those assets which are expected to be consumed or realised in the ordinary course of business in the short term.

3. The precise nature of the asset is not the only criterion as regards classification. Assets considered to be 'fixed' in one business would not necessarily be so in another.

4. When valuers are asked to make a valuation whether it be of land and buildings or plant and machinery for inclusion in a company's accounts (whether by incorporating the valuation in the accounts or by a reference in a note or in the directors' report) it is essential that there should be a clear understanding by all concerned of what is being valued and the date of the valuation. Valuation reports and certificates should clearly define inclusions and exclusions. It is also essential that there should be a clear understanding of the basis of valuation and the proposed treatment of that valuation in the accounts, etc., in order to ensure that there is a proper comparison between the valuation and the book amount of the same assets. Unless this understanding exists between the directors, the accountants and the valuers concerned, there is always the risk that misleading comparisons will be drawn.

101

Basis of Valuation

1. (a) Basic accounting concepts postulate that accounts are on a going concern basis, that is to say that the enterprise will continue in operational existence for the foreseeable future. The normal basis of valuation of plant and machinery where the valuation is to be incorporated or referred to in the accounts, etc., of a company should therefore be its open market value on the assumption that the plant and machinery will continue in its present existing use in the business of the company. Normally this existing use basis of valuation will be depreciated replacement cost, i.e., the estimated cost as new at the date of the valuation including the cost of installation less an allowance for depreciation (i.e., wear and tear, age and obsolescence). Account should be taken in the valuation, however, of special factors such as scarcity value or the possible limitation of value caused by limited natural resources or the building housing the plant having a limited life or being held on a limited tenure or with limited planning consent. Further it is necessary to consider both individual and overall values of the plant.

    (b) In some cases an existing use basis of valuation will not be appropriate. It would almost certainly be inappropriate to use an existing use basis of valuation of plant and machinery where land and the buildings in which they are housed are valued on an alternative use basis. When reference is made to a valuation of land and buildings on an alternative use basis, (see Guidance Notes on the Valuation of Company Property Assets dated February 1974 (Guidance Note A,2)) consideration needs to be given to the effect on the value of plant and machinery. In these circumstances the following alternatives would be available:–

    (i) where the plant and machinery could be moved to and used by the company at another site, the valuation would be on a depreciated replacement cost basis, but making an allowance for the costs of removal and reinstallation;

    (ii) where plant and machinery is to be disposed of rather than used in the company's business it would then be valued on an open market value basis. If there is a time limit on the disposal, forced sale value may be the proper basis of valuation.

2. Where the land and buildings have not been valued, then the plant and machinery should be valued on the basis that would have been appropriate had the land and buildings been valued.

3. Definitions of open market value and forced sale value are given in Annex 'A' to these Guidance Notes. These definitions are to be used for the purpose of valuations which are to be used in company accounts, etc., and they cannot override any statutory definitions of market value which may have to be adopted for the purpose of valuation for capital gains tax, compensation cases, etc.

4. In all instances, it is essential that, in advance of the valuation being carried out, there should be a clear understanding with the company and its accountants (and probably its auditors) of what is to be valued, the reasons for the valuation, the use to be made of the valuation and all the surrounding circumstances so that the appropriate basis can be determined.

Plant and Machinery forming part of a Building

1. Problems have arisen when valuing land and buildings where there are items of plant and machinery which are regarded by the valuer as forming part of the building but which the accountant may wish to segregate for accounting purposes. Valuers when valuing premises will normally include all items of plant and machinery on the premises which provide the services to the land and buildings and which the open market regards as an integral part of the premises for letting or sale or as security for a loan.

2. A list of such items is given in Annex 'B' to these Guidance Notes but it is stressed that the list is not comprehensive and merely indicates, as a general guide to valuers, those items that would usually fall to be included in the value of the premises.

3. Normally process plant and machinery should not be included in the valuation of the premises.

4. It is possible that some or all of these types of plant and machinery normally included in the valuation of the premises may be needed to be separated for accounting purposes, for instance when it is expected that they have a shorter useful life than the rest of the premises and depreciation is being provided accordingly.

5. Valuers may from time to time be asked to split a valuation which they have made of premises between (i) Land and Buildings and (ii) the plant and machinery element in order to correspond with the headings adopted by the company in its accounts.

6. In such circumstances valuers will have to indicate clearly that their valuation is of the whole and it is not practicable to arrive at separate valuations of the individual components. Nevertheless, valuers may be able to assist in suggesting ways of allocating their overall valuation between the different components. Valuers should clearly state in their report, and it should be explained in any reference thereto in the company accounts, that the valuation is an overall valuation and any split between the components is only an allocation of amounts to the components within the overall valuation figure. It is recommended that such allocation of amounts should be contained not in the main report but in a covering letter.

Dies, Moulds, Patterns and Spare Parts

1. As a general rule, dies, moulds, patterns, jigs, drawings, designs and similar items should be excluded from a valuation.

2. In the normal course of events, spare parts would not be valued as part of the unit as it is often the practice for these to be carried in stock, and only auxiliary items necessary for the operation of the unit would be included in the valuation.

3. In both cases, valuers should consult with the directors and auditors in order to take the appropriate action.

Plant and Machinery Register

1. It is recommended that all companies be encouraged to maintain an up-to-date plant and machinery register showing as a minimum, the location of each item of plant and machinery, its date of acquisition, original cost and any further capital expenditure as this assists considerably in a valuation and its reconciliation with the company accounts.

General

1. Valuers are advised to discuss with the Company Accountants and Auditors the requirements of the valuation before carrying out the detailed valuation.

2. Reports and certificates should incorporate suitable savings clauses covering the treatment in the valuation of such items as assets on hire purchase, government grants and goodwill.

Consent

1. The Valuer's Certificate should state that his written consent to any reference to his valuation in company accounts and/or directors' reports or any company statement or circular must be obtained before such documents are published. All Valuation Certificates should, therefore, incorporate a paragraph to the effect that:—

'Neither the whole nor any part of this Valuation Certificate or any reference thereto may be included in any published document, circular or statement nor published in any way without the Valuer's written approval of the form and context in which it may appear.'

Annex 'A'

PLANT AND MACHINERY
DEFINITION OF THE OPEN MARKET VALUE AND THE FORCED SALE VALUE

The **Open Market Value** is defined as the best price at which an interest in the plant and machinery might reasonably be expected to be sold at the date of valuation by either Private Treaty, Public Auction or Tender, as may be appropriate assuming:

(a) a willing seller;

(b) a reasonable period within which to negotiate the sale, taking into account the nature of the plant and machinery and the state of the market;

(c) values will remain static throughout the period;

(d) the plant and machinery will be freely exposed to the market;

(e) no account is to be taken of an additional bid by a special purchaser;

(f) the plant and machinery may be valued, either

    (i) as a whole in its working place, or

    (ii) as individual items for removal.

The **Forced Sale Value** is defined as the open market value (as defined in the above paragraph) with the proviso that the vendor has imposed a time limit for completion which cannot be regarded as a reasonable period as referred to in (b) above.

PLANT AND MACHINERY
ITEMS OF PLANT AND MACHINERY NORMALLY INCLUDED
BY SURVEYORS IN VALUATIONS OF LAND AND BUILDINGS

Note

The following observations are intended to apply in the valuation of assets comprised in the majority of industrial and commercial types of property. Factory premises of a specialised nature will often require individual treatment and segregation to meet particular circumstances. In the case of sale, fire insurance, rating, etc., different criteria may apply. The list which follows, however, whilst not comprehensive, indicates those items usually valued on the basis that they form part of the 'building' service installations as opposed to those provided as part of the industrial or commercial processes carried on by the occupier. It follows that the valuation of land and buildings would normally exclude all items of plant, machinery and equipment which may have been installed wholly or primarily in connection with the occupiers' industrial or commercial processes, furniture and furnishings, tenants' fixtures and fittings, vehicles, stock, moulds and loose tools. The excluded items may need to be separately valued for balance sheet or other purposes.

Electricity

Mains supply cables, transformer houses with transformers, sub-stations and their equipment, generating plant and associated equipment including standby plant, and all wiring and switchgear up to and including the main distribution board in each building, together with:–

(a) *In non-industrial buildings*
Wiring for lighting and power from the distribution board to wall and ceiling points.

(b) *In industrial buildings*
Wiring for lighting to wall and ceiling points.
Note: (power circuits from the distribution board would normally be excluded on the grounds that these are related to the processes).

(c) *Externally*
Wiring and associated structures for lighting to roads and yards, etc.

Gas

Gas mains up to and including meter houses and piping from meter houses for non-process purposes. Where the property includes a gas producer plant this would normally be in connection with the occupier's industrial processes and would, therefore, be excluded.

Water

Wells, boreholes, pumps, pump houses, service pipes including those connected to Water Board's mains, water treatment plants, storage tanks and reservoirs and all structures required to contain, support or house such items.

Space Heating and Hot Water

Boilers and associated plant including fuel tanks, pipes and fittings (e.g., radiators and unit fan heaters) primarily supplying or using steam or hot water for space heating and other non-process purposes.

Independent space heating units and hot water fittings in the nature of 'landlords' fittings.

105

Air Conditioning and Ventilation

Air conditioning plant and trunking and fan extractors and ventilators except where forming part of a computer installation or primarily serving plant and machinery used in industrial or commercial processes.

Fire and Security

Hydrants, pumps and mains, sprinkler systems, smoke detectors and annexed fire and burglar alarm systems.

Drainage

Surface water and foul water drains and sewers.

Sewage disposal plants not primarily concerned with treating water and other liquids used in the processes or trade effluents.

Lifts and Gantries

Passenger and goods lifts, escalators and travelators designed to benefit the general occupation of a building.

Rails and supporting gantries for overhead travelling cranes where forming an integral part of the structure of a building.

Note:

Hoists, conveyors, elevators, overhead cranes, jib and derrick cranes would normally be excluded.

Structures

The decision upon which items should be included will, to some extent, depend upon general experience and the practice adopted by individual trades.

Among the criteria will be the degree of attachment, permanence and size. Structures which are necessary for the provision of the services or have been installed or erected other than for the industrial or commercial processes carried out on the property would normally be included in the valuation of land and buildings. Such items might include the following:—

Boiler houses, Chimneys (brick and steel) and Economiser Chambers
Pits
Stagings
Internal Buildings
Permanent Partitions
Railways
Bridges and Housings for Conveyors
Fences
Roads, Yards and Hard Standings
Structures which are ancillary to, or form a part of an item of Plant and Machinery, would normally be excluded.

Appendix 6

Stock Exchange Listing Agreement

Preliminary

1. This chapter is divided into two sections which deal with information required in prospectuses and circulars issued by property companies. Section A concerns companies no part of whose capital is already listed. Section B concerns companies already having listed securities.

   These requirements are intended to cover primarily property investment and property development companies. Where property dealing companies are concerned, some difference of treatment may be necessary according to the circumstances of each case.

   A specimen valuation certificate is set out at the end of this Chapter. It is a guide and there may be occasions which merit some variation in detail. The Royal Institution of Chartered Surveyors ("the RICS") has published a manual of "Guidance Notes on the Valuation of Assets" and the Council of The Stock Exchange suggest that any valuer would be likely to find this manual helpful.

Schedule II Part A of Appendix
Pages 186 to 195

Initial applications

Section A
Companies no part of whose share or loan capital is already listed

2. A valuation of the freehold and leasehold properties of the company or the group (as the case may be) together with the name of the valuer, his address and any professional qualification and the date of his valuation, is required to be included in the prospectus

of a company no part of whose share or loan capital is already listed. The valuation should state the effective date as at which the properties were valued. If such date is not the same as that to which the final balance sheet is made up in the accountant's report it may be necessary for the prospectus to include particulars of the reconciliation between the valuation figure and the figure included in the final balance sheet. A property should not be included in the valuation unless the legal estate is beneficially vested in the Company or the Group.

Where the directors have required a valuation of the benefit or detriment of contractural arrangements in respect of property, or where there is thought to be benefit in any options held, such valuations should be shown quite separately and should include, *inter alia*, a reconciliation of the costs and values.

Independence of valuer

3. The valuer must, unless otherwise approved by the Department, be an external valuer (as defined in the guidance notes published by the RICS), and have an appropriate professional qualification. He should not be either a director or an employee of the company or any of its subsidiaries or in partnership with or employed by such a director or employee. A partnership or a company may not act as valuer if any of its partners or directors would be so disqualified. The Council will be prepared to consider waiving the necessity for an external valuation, (as defined in the guidance notes published by the RICS), in cases where companies maintain a qualified surveyor's department.

Particulars of properties to be included in valuations

4. The following particulars should be included in the valuation report in respect of each property:—

(a) the address;

(b) a brief description (e.g., land or buildings, approximate area, etc.);

(c) existing use (e.g., shops, offices, factories, residential, etc.);

(d) tenure (i.e., freehold, or leasehold, giving term);

108

(e) terms of tenants' leases or underleases (including repairing obligations);

(f) approximate age of the buildings;

(g) present capital value in existing state;

(h) property occupied by the group should be identified and the terms of any intra-group lease granted by a parent company to a subsidiary should be stated;

(i) any other matters which materially affect the value.

If the properties held are too numerous to enable all such particulars to be given without undue length, the Department should be consulted. In some cases suitable condensed details may be acceptable. In other cases it may be acceptable to have a detailed valuation report available for inspection, and a summarised valuation report included in the prospectus.

Basis of valuation to be stated

5. (a) The valuation report must state whether the valuation is based on open market value, or, if necessary, depreciated replacement cost subject to adequate profitability.

(b) Where the valuation is in respect of land currently being developed or with development potential the following additional information should be given:—

(i) whether planning consent has been obtained and, if so, the date and whether there are any conditions attached to such consent;

(ii) the date when the development is expected to be completed and any estimate of letting or occupation dates;

(iii) the estimated total cost of carrying out the development including the cost of financial carrying charges, letting commissions, etc., or (where part of the development has already been carried out) the estimated cost of completing the development similarly;

109

(iv) the estimated capital value of the property in the open market in its present condition; and

(v) the estimated capital values after development has been completed and after completion and letting of the property.

6. There shall be included in the valuation report in respect of each property:— **Rentals used in valuation**

(a) estimated current net annual rental. This means the income which is estimated by the valuer to be the current net annual income (ignoring any special receipts or deductions) arising from the property before tax on profits and any allowance for interest on capital or loans but after making deductions for superior rents (but not for any amortization) and all disbursements including the expenses of managing the property and appropriate annual allowances to maintain it in a condition to continue to command its rent.

(b) estimated future net annual rental at named date (where this differs materially from the current net rental); and a statement whether such information is based on current rental values.

Where rentals are referred to in a valuation report, it should state whether they are based on present day market rental values, or, if not, the basis adopted.

7. In cases in which directors or promoters have been interested in any acquisition or disposal of any of the properties during the two years preceding the valuation there must be disclosed either in the valuation report, or elsewhere in the prospectus, particulars of such interests together with *(a)* the nature of their interest, *(b)* the dates of the transactions, and *(c)* the prices paid or received, or other terms on which the transactions were effected. **Interests of directors or promoters**

110

Summary

8. In a summary in the valuation report the number of properties and their aggregate current value should be split to show the separate totals for the freehold and leasehold properties. Where the number of properties held is too large for paragraph 4 to be applied, a more elaborate summary may be required in lieu, according to the circumstances.

Specimen valuation

9. A specimen valuation which would be generally suitable in a variety of circumstances is set out at the end of this chapter.

Schedule II Part B Appendix

Section B

Companies part of whose share or loan capital is already listed

Acquisitions

10. In the case of a further issue of securities, whether for cash or as vendor consideration, and also in cases of acquisitions out of the company's resources, including borrowings, a valuation of the properties being acquired will not necessarily be called for unless the acquisitions are substantial in relation to the existing properties of the company or there are circumstances which, in the opinion of the Council, justify the inclusion of a valuation (e.g., where the directors or controlling shareholders are interested in the transaction). In such a case the circular must give information about the acquisitions including details of the properties acquired or about to be acquired, details of the consideration, the effect on profits of the acquisition, the current indebtedness including terms of loans raised since the last published accounts and other information required to be disclosed by Schedule II, Part B, of the Appendix, and must be approved by the Department. A substantial acquisition in this context is one by which the net book value, or published valuation, of the properties owned by the acquiring company, before deducting mortgages, has, as a result of the acquisition or acquisitions, increased by 20% or more.

111

In the case of acquisitions of properties having a value which is small in relation to the existing properties of the company, any press announcement must include a general description of the property acquired and be in a form approved by the Department.

The Department must be informed of the names of the vendors, whether or not this information will be disclosed in the circular or announcement.

General requirements with regard to acquisitions and realisations appear in Chapter 4 on pages 65 to 75.

11. Where a listed property company enters into a sale and leaseback transaction with another party to finance the development of a property or properties representing a substantial part of the company's portfolio, full details of the terms of such transaction and the financial arrangements must be included in a circular to shareholders. Such a circular must set out details of the stake taken in the development and in subsequent income by the other party, so that shareholders are aware of the effect of the transaction on the assets and income of their company. Substantial in this context means 20% of the net book value or published valuation of the listed company's properties, before deducting mortgages. **Sale and leaseback transactions**

12. A listed property company in receipt of a bid for its shares or for part of its assets or undertaking may in certain circumstances be justified in publishing in addition to a valuation of its properties or developments in their existing state some indication of prospective values. Such an indication of future value would require a number of assumptions to be made and these should be stated; if any such publication is proposed the Department should be consulted at an early stage. **Bid situations**

SPECIMEN VALUATION CERTIFICATE

Date.........19....

To the Directors.

....Co. Ltd.

The Preamble

The Valuer **should set out in a suitable form of preamble all matters** which normally would be included in a report and valuation to a client. This can be in an abbreviated style but **no material item, not mentioned in the rest of the Certificate, should be omitted.**

The preamble should include a statement of the date and basis of valuation and matters related thereto. If third parties have provided the Valuer with information on which he is relying he should state their sources and the nature of the information——e.g. details of tenures, use and lettings and, where appropriate, building and site areas, town planning **consents or similar detail.**

It should be stated whether or not any allowances have been made in the valuation for the expenses of realisation or taxation (e.g. Capital Gains or Development Land Taxes), and it may be appropriate to indicate whether or not structural surveys of buildings and inspections of service installations and machinery have been carried out and as to the general state of repair.

Where a matter concerns one property only it may be better to include it in a notated footnote to that particular schedule.

[Non-publication without consent clause.]

A. Properties held as investments

Property	Description, age and tenure	Terms of tenants' leases or underleases	Estimated net annual current rental before tax	Present capital value in existing state
			£	£
1. No. 26, William Street, London, S.W.3.	7 shops with 6 maisonettes over. Freehold. Built about 1965.	Shop leases expire in 1991; maisonettes on 3-year agreements and on regulated tenancies. Shops full repairing and insuring leases. maisonettes internal repairing and insuring leases. Rent reviews on shops in 1986.	6,700	79,000
2. No. 16, Bagnall Row, London, S.W.1.	30 flats and 16 garages. Leasehold. 63 years unexpired at annual fixed ground rent of £900. Built about 1937.	16 unfurnished flats and 14 furnished flats, the former on 3-year agreements and on regulated tenancies, the latter each for one year. Garages let quarterly. Landlords responsible for internal and external repairs. Unfurnished tenants refund cost of services.	20,800	151,000
3. Parrey House, Hanover Square, London. W.1.	Offices having about 20,100 sq. ft. of floor space. Leasehold having about 83 years unexpired at annual ground rent of £3,000 with one fixed increase to £4,000 in 1998. Built about 1956.	2 leases for 21 years, both full repairing and insuring leases expiring in 1986, with a rent review in 1981.	160,000	2,300,000
4. No. 7, Lloyd Street, London, E.1	Warehouse having about 10,000 sq. ft. of floor space in post-war trading estate. Leasehold, 41 years unexpired at an annual ground rent of £800 without reviews.	Full repairing and insuring lease for 14 years expiring in 1990, with a rent review in 1985.	3,500	32,000
				£2,562,000

114

B. Properties being developed

Property	Description, age and tenure	Tenancies arranged	Present capital value in existing state	Estimated completion and occupation dates	Estimated cost of completing development	Estimated Net annual rental before tax	Capital value when completed	Capital value when completed and let
5. Site of Odeon Cinema, Wilmslow, Cheshire.	Cleared Site. Freehold.	Site let to the Waldorf Co. Ltd. for 99 years for development as an hotel with shops on the ground floor & a basement car park. Rent review each 7 years to 1/10th rental value.	£ 50,000	—	£ —	£ 5,000	£	£ 60,000
6. 10, Sydney Road, Ealing, London, W.5.	Office block having about 20,000 sq. ft. floor space on ground and 5 upper floors, with basement car park. Leasehold, about 97 years unexpired at annual ground rent of £25,000 with rent reviews each 5 years to 1/5th rental value.	Let on lease for whole term to the English Television Authority. Rent reviews every 5 years.	583,000	Completion 1/6/82 Occupation 1/9/82	253,000	90,000		1,165,000
7. 18/40 (e), Great South Road, Lewisham, London, S.E.13.	A freehold office building having about 100,000 sq. ft. in a 10 storey block with 12 shops below and car park for 60 cars reaching completion.	3 shop units let to Cheapways Supermarket Limited. 9 shop units let to non-multiple traders. Shop leases are on full repairing and insuring terms for 20 years with rent reviews every 5 years. 10,000 sq. ft. of offices let to Great South Road Insurance Limited upon a 20 year internal repairing lease with rent reviews every 5 years and with a proportionate contribution towards all landlords' expenses of servicing and maintaining the building.	1,810,000	Completion 1/9/82 Occupation 1/3/83	60,000	175,000	1,870,000	2,244,000
			£2,443,000		£313,000			£3,470,000

115

C. Properties held for development in the future

Property	Description, age and tenure	Terms of existing tenants' leases or underleases	Estimated current net annual rental before tax	Present capital value in existing state
			£	£
8. 21, Belinda Walk, London, W.2.	9 flats and 8 garages. Leasehold, 21 years unexpired at an annual ground rent of £600 (a).	Leases expire between 1979 and 1984. Garages let quarterly.	2,900	15,000
9. 16, Ditton Road, Sunbury-on-Thames.	Private house with site of about 30,000 sq. ft. Freehold (b).	Held on one lease expiring in 1983.	600	22,000
10. 196/305 (incl.) Upper Kings Road, including area bounded by Chepstow Street and Elmhurst Road, London, S.W.1.	196 shops, offices and houses occupying a site of about 3 acres. Leasehold, 120 years unexpired at an annual ground rent of £3,000 (c).	All ground leases expire in 1981.	3,920	1,210,000
11. 22/44 Riverside, Battersea.	12 private houses. Leasehold, 99 years unexpired at an annual ground rent of £7,500 with reviews to 1/8th of rental value each 33 years (d).	All leases expire in 1984.	Deficit of £1,650	360,000
				£1,607,000

Notes: (a) Negotiations are in hand for a new ground lease, conditional on redevelopment being undertaken.

(b) Planning permission was given for 10 maisonettes on 3/8/78.

(c) Application for town planning consent has not yet been made. The ground rent is to be increased to £25,000 in 1987 but fixed thereafter.

(d) The site is clearly ripe for redevelopment. Outline planning consent for 60 flats has been granted on 12/12/78.

116

D. Properties held for disposal

Property	Description, age and tenure	Terms of existing tenants' leases or underleases	Estimated current net annual rental before tax	Present capital value in existing state
			£	£
12. Mayfair Trading Estate, Barchester.	6 acres. Freehold site for industrial development (e).	none	—	115,000
13. Backlands Farm, Corrington, Wilts.	7·6 acres. Freehold site for part of a large residential estate (f).	A 12 month licence to occupy certain part of the premises.	400	90,000
14. Noview Estate, Frodsham, Surrey	11·4 acres. Freehold site zoned for residential uses. (g)	none	—	180,000
15. 12/20 York Road, Gorston	Freehold office building of 20,000 sq. ft. Built 1960.	none	—	300,000
				£685,000

(e) Detailed planning consent granted on 6/2/78 to one factory of 10,000 sq. ft. Remainder of land zoned for industrial use.

(f) Detailed planning consent for 30 houses, granted on 11/9/78.

(g) Detailed planning consent for 40 houses, granted on 15/11/78.

SUMMARY

Present Capital Value

Freehold
8 Properties £3,090,000

Leasehold
7 Properties £5,234,000

£8,324,000

We are, Gentlemen,

Yours faithfully.

10 Court Lane, London, E.C.4.

117

Appendix 7

List of those attending seminar

Dearden Farrow

Pat Young

Bob Crossley

Jo Holden

Jeremy Hopkinson

Malcolm Penney

Tony Reed

Hamish Renton

John Surrey

Pat Townend

Richard Ellis

D.N. Idris Pearce

John Borner

Ken Ceasar

Mike Dix

Martin Farr

John Hibbert

Alastair Pringle

Tim Roberton

Mike de Vick

Chairman

C. A. Westwick, London School of Economics

Index

120